DIGITAL MARKETING ESSENTIALS

YOU ALWAYS WANTED TO KNOW

VIBRANT
PUBLISHERS

Digital Marketing Essentials

You Always Wanted To Know

Paperback ISBN 10: 1-949395-74-X
Paperback ISBN 13: 978-1-949395-74-7

Ebook ISBN 10: 1-949395-42-1
Ebook ISBN 13: 978-1-949395-42-6

Hardback ISBN 10: 1-949395-43-X
Hardback ISBN 13: 978-1-949395-43-3

Library of Congress Control Number: 2020938729

This publication is designed to provide accurate and authoritative information in regard to the subject matter covered. The Author has made every effort in the preparation of this book to ensure the accuracy of the information. However, information in this book is sold without warranty either expressed or implied. The Author or the Publisher will not be liable for any damages caused or alleged to be caused either directly or indirectly by this book.

Vibrant Publishers books are available at special quantity discount for sales promotions, or for use in corporate training programs. For more information please write to bulkorders@vibrantpublishers.com

Please email feedback / corrections (technical, grammatical or spelling) to spellerrors@vibrantpublishers.com

To access the complete catalogue of Vibrant Publishers, visit www.vibrantpublishers.com

What experts say about this book!

Digital Marketing Essentials You Always Wanted to Know is a fantastic addition to the field.

As an MBA Professor that has worked with hundreds of students and local businesses around their marketing challenges, many have no clue what is meant by the term "digital marketing" or how it differs from "traditional" marketing.

Let me be perfectly clear here – I see digital as part of the P called PROMOTION and it makes me sick that so many in my profession are entirely focused on that one thing. It is critical you know how to do digital more effectively.

Reading this book is as if you are sharing a meal with an expert who, as each course is brought to the table, addresses every digital marketing fundamental you must know and understand. Email, SEO, metrics, advertising, conversion rates etc. are all covered.

It will get you "up to speed" quickly and give you a jump-off point to start executing the tactics.

Highly recommended for any student looking to "level-up" their understanding of this critical marketing topic.

    – Thomas Elmer. MBA

    MARKETING MUSCLE. LLC

    Adjunct Professor - West Chester University and Cairn University

What experts say about this book!

Digital Marketing Essentials is an essential book for digital marketers and educators. A comprehensive straight to the point guide providing a clear view on digital marketing techniques and framework on what works for beginners to experts alike. An up to date mixture of modern and traditional views on digital marketing that is easy to understand with clear concepts and examples.

– Eric Lui
Professor at New York University & Baruch College
Advisory Board Member - Pace University

If you're looking for a well-organized and well-written book on the fundamentals of digital marketing, this book is for you. I'm always on the look-out for new marketing textbooks for my university students across the country, so I was pleasantly surprised when I came across this book. It's a rock solid introduction to some of the most important concepts in marketing today. Best of all, it focuses on the practical application of digital marketing, not just on the academic theory. Bravo!

– Jamie Turner
Internationally Recognized Author, Speaker and University Lecturer

What experts say about this book!

In Digital Marketing Essentials, the publisher has simplified the self-learning digital marketing fundamentals in an easy-to-understand language for any learner. The book discusses the traditional and modern methods to apply in modern marketing with comparison, and advantages of the modern process. It illustrates how a business owner can grow his/her business with a range of topics such as SEO, online advertising, email marketing, social media, Amazon, Google, e-Commerce, and so much more. You learn how a modern marketer can manage a business from the comfort of his or her own space yet, expands it to the world.

In each chapter, the book introduces the learner on how to apply smart content combined with the strategic advertisement, marketing campaigns, or positioning of the content products applying various strategies. Following the lessons, the modern marketer gains the leverage to be unique and educated about the market with an outstanding business plan, recognize the trends, metrics while supplying the demand yet keeping up with a different variety of traffics.

– Afsaneh Mardani
Adjunct Professor
City University of New York

The textbook is well-written and should give students a good working knowledge of terminology, theory, and practice for implementing digital strategy.

– Joe Stabb, Ph.D.,
Assistant Professor
Oswego State University of New York

BUY 3 FOR THE PRICE OF 2

USE DISCOUNT CODE 3FOR2

*Discount applies to the lowest value item.

Cannot be combined with other offers | Offer valid till stocks last | Offer valid only on

www.vibrantpublishers.com

Table of Contents

This page is intentionally left blank

Introduction

This guide is full of strategies and insights on key concepts of digital marketing for those people who are just starting or want to hone their digital marketing skills and be updated on the latest digital marketing trends and tactics. If you also wish to take your business online successfully, this is the right guide for you.

In today's world, digital marketing influences the buying behavior of a consumer. Digital marketing now dictates how consumers make purchasing decisions when buying products or services. Because of this effectiveness, digital marketing has become a must for any business trying to compete in the modern market, regardless of the type or size of the industry.

It's paramount for companies and business owners to understand how digital marketing works, so they can strategically use the right digital techniques and campaigning tactics to reach and engage their targeted audience.

Although digital marketing is rapidly evolving, the underlying core concepts and principles remain the same. These concepts and principles have emerged as the building blocks of digital marketing all over the world, and this guide tries to examine and explain them in finer details.

This page is intentionally left blank

Chapter 1

Understanding Digital Marketing

D igital Marketing is a collective term for the marketing of services and products through digital technologies, largely the internet, but also including advertisements, mobile phones, and many other digital channels.

The evolving nature of digital marketing since the 1990s has changed the way firms and brands use digital marketing and technology for marketing. Today, digital marketing is the phenomenon that unites customization and mass distribution to achieve marketing goals.

Digital marketing campaigns are becoming more and more predominant and effective, as digital platforms continue being integrated into our everyday marketing plans, and as people stop going to physical shops and instead use digital devices.

The unique convergence of technology and the multiplication of digital devices has brought about new digital marketing strategies that offer much potential to organizations and brands. Such strategies include public relations, marketing automation, branding, visual communication, relevant advertising, measuring output, and many others.

Digital marketing such as search engine marketing, social media optimization, content marketing, social media marketing, search engine optimization (SEO), display advertising, and influencer marketing is very common in our advancing technology. It's extending to other non-internet-based channels that offer digital media, like a callback, on-hold mobile ringtones, and mobile phones (SMS and MMS).

In this chapter, we will learn

- To define and understand both traditional and digital marketing

- How digital marketing works

- The overall digital marketing process

- The movement of customers through the digital marketing funnel

1.1 Traditional Marketing vs. Digital Marketing

The debate on finding the most effective marketing approach still rages on, but amid all these debates, some interesting questions relating to digital marketing and traditional marketing are arising. Is digital marketing a modern version of traditional marketing? Which is the most beneficial approach between digital marketing and traditional marketing? Finally, which marketing strategy is most preferred by companies?

To answer these lingering questions, we must understand how traditional marketing and digital marketing compare to each other, and what the differences in their characteristics are.

"Marketing is the process of executing and planning the pricing, promotion, distributions, and conception of goods, services, and ideas to create an exchange that satisfies the individual and organization objectives"- **Philip Kotler**

Traditional Marketing

Traditional marketing pertains to older media: prints, broadcasts, direct mails, telephones and billboards, point of purchase (POP), and face-to-face. Traditional marketing was the only form of marketing until the creation of the Internet in 1990.

This marketing strategy might have evolved over the years, but the fundamental aspects remain intact. The marketing techniques we utilize today still depend heavily on the four Ps of marketing. That is the product, price, place, and promotion.

On the outside, digital marketing might seem so different from traditional marketing because it's all about the fourth P, "promotion." But the fact is that digital marketing wouldn't be so efficient if it wasn't depending on the other Ps. Digital marketing uses each P in its own unique way, which is sometimes even better than the way traditional marketing uses them.

Digital Marketing

The digital marketing goal is the same as that of traditional marketing, to engage customers and address their concerns.

Digital marketing allows for stronger and in-depth analysis of Customer Relationship management that wasn't possible with traditional marketing. With a simple profile and dialogue, a company can get more insights of each consumer and fragment the market more deeply to suit their needs and desires.

1.2 Traditional Marketing vs. Digital Marketing: The Differences

The Reach of the Marketing Approach

Even though traditional marketing is still efficient, it depends on targeting and finding customers grounded on demographics, while digital marketing puts companies out in the opening for people to find them.

Ease of Access

One downside to digital marketing is that, unlike the traditional marketing methods where ads are carried on easily understandable and accessible channels like magazines, daily newspapers, radio jingles, and street displays, it depends on the ease of its potential customers to access the Internet and be familiar to the channels being used to target them. When there is no connection or knowledge of using digital channels, the adverts won't reach the targeted customers.

Inability to Target and Monitor Your Campaign Performance

Unlike traditional marketing, digital marketing provides companies with tools that help in monitoring campaign performance and measuring its effects. It allows them to track their website traffic effortlessly.

Limited Interaction

In digital marketing, there is limited interaction between the customer and the platform used for marketing. Traditional marketing, on the other hand, is a one-way street where companies can provide or broadcast their product or service information to the targeted audience directly. The main aim of this brand-building process is to target a certain group of potential customers and convert them.

Traditional marketing methods like face-to-face marketing gives companies a chance to obtain real-time feedback, which is insightful when you are testing out a new product.

Higher Costs

It might cost you a lot more to reserve small space in the local newspaper or air-time on one of the TV stations or local radio stations than posting an advert on YouTube or Facebook. The high recurring costs associated with investing in traditional marketing might not give the returns you desire.

Digital marketing offers you the chance to create multiple campaigns at the same time and on a budget that suits your needs. You can target several people in different countries, or different ages and genders. Also, you can evaluate and edit your advertisements to adapt to the different market changes, incurring no extra costs.

Return on Investment (ROI)

Digital marketing stands out as the best choice to measure and increase ROI than traditional marketing because of the availability of different online analytical platforms.

1.3 How Digital Marketing Works

Defining digital marketing is easy but understanding how it works is a bit complicated. We have already clarified that digital marketing is all about using digital platforms and digital channels for business marketing and promotion. But, as a digital marketer, you need to understand its importance and how it works.

Digital marketing is neither a product nor a service that works for you; it's a concept you have to adapt and make it work for you. Confusing, right? Don't worry, when we are done with this section, everything will be crystal clear.

Digital marketing works through integrating digital channels like Facebook, Google, and YouTube with marketing techniques such as Pay Per Click (PPC), E-mail Marketing, Social Media Marketing, and many others to draw and bring around customers.

The whole idea behind this process is to identify and target potential customers and interest them with what you are offering, finally convincing them to purchase and subscribe to your channel.

But first, you need to set a goal: what do you aim to achieve with digital marketing? Different marketing strategies and platforms suit different forms of advertisement. For brand awareness, social media marketing can be perfect. But if you want to create leads, PPC and SEO might be what you need.

Now that you understand that digital marketing can work in different ways depending on your ultimate business or marketing goal, let us see what digital marketing comprises.

The Digital Marketing Process

There are various digital technologies that businesses and marketers can use to broadcast their marketing messages to their targeted audience. Examples of technologies that can attract and engage prospects include mobile technology (social media, smartphones), PPC, e-mail marketing, and display ads.

In this era, digital marketing plays a significant role in how consumers make purchasing decisions. It's therefore important for companies to take their business online and boost their online visibility as much as possible.

Gone are the days when customers would go to a physical shop to purchase or get information on products or services. Now, consumers utilize the Internet to obtain information on various products and make knowledgeable purchasing verdicts; even if they'll visit a physical shop, it might be to get their product or complete the purchase.

This is where digital marketing comes in: it helps your company reach your targeted customer wherever they are in their customer value journey.

Digital Marketing Funnel

This is a virtual representation of the stages a customer goes through from the very first time they are introduced to a product until when they make a purchase and become customers.

1. Your targeted audience becomes informed of your brand or product.

2. It sparks an interest in them, so they go to your social media platform or official website to learn more on the product.

3. They sign up, make an inquiry, or add the product to the cart.

4. They may purchase the product. If they don't, it might be because of some uncertainty and you might have to re-evaluate your marketing strategy.

5. Finally, they buy the product and become your client.

Depending on your business type, **digital marketing funnels** can be categorized into three levels:

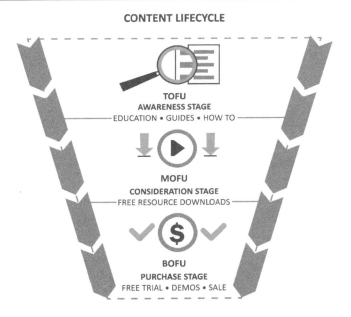

Top of the Funnel(TOFU)

This is the awareness stage. This stage uses multiple digital marketing channels to boost your brand or product visibility to your targeted audience.

Middle of the Funnel (MOFU)

This is the stage where your targeted customers are already in the funnel and deciding whether to purchase your product. Their decision depends entirely on various factors, such as your website speed, the prices offered by your competitors, and the shipping fee.

Bottom of the Funnel (BOFU)

This is the final stage or the converting stage. Your potential customers have decided on purchasing your brand or products, and if you guarantee them better offers, discounts, and quick delivery options, your chance of conversion will increase and the sale can happen.

Digital Marketing Techniques

Digital marketing techniques differ greatly from digital marketing channels. A digital marketing technique is using digital marketing channels to promote your brands or products.

You can use paid marketing in Facebook Ad and Google Ad channels to increase traffic on your business site and generate leads.

Here is a list of digital marketing techniques:

- Search Engine Optimization (SEO)
- Video and Display Marketing
- Blogging
- Content Marketing
- Re-targeting and Remarketing
- Digital Advertisement
- Paid Advertisement
- E-mail Marketing
- Mobile Marketing
- Affiliate Marketing

- Marketing Automation

- Influencer Marketing

- Social Media Marketing

- Digital Public Relations

Digital Marketing Channels

Digital channels are platforms that allow communication between you and your targeted customers to promote your brand or product. You can use digital marketing strategies on multiple channels to promote a single marketing campaign.

Figure 1.2

DIGITAL MARKETING INFOGRAPHIC

BASIC CHANNELS	LATEST DEVELOPMENT AND STRATEGIES
Affiliate marketing	Influencer marketing
Display advertising	Remarketing
Email marketing	Collaboration
SEM	Game advertising
SEO	Confidential advertising	OBA
SMM	50% people in Internet
Active approach	75% on social media
Passive approach	25% mobile presence
Online PR	Video advertising

With the help of digital marketing channels, you can boost the efficiency and visibility of your marketing campaign. By being available in all digital marketing channels, you can boost your brand credibility among your targeted customers.

Below is a list of some of the most common digital marketing channels:

- YouTube: Video Marketing

- Google Ads: Paid Marketing

- E-mail Marketing

- Social Media: Instagram, LinkedIn, Facebook Ads

- Google Search Engine: Organic Marketing

- Digital Advertisement Channels: Display Ads

- WhatsApp and SMS

1.3.1 Digital Marketing Objectives

Before working on anything else, first state your digital marketing objectives. Ensure that it covers a broad spectrum of everything you want from your digital marketing campaign. Besides, your objectives should be in line with your ultimate marketing or business goals.

In simple terms, your objectives should be SMART.

Figure 1.3

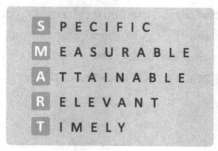

GOAL SETTING

S PECIFIC

M EASURABLE

A TTAINABLE

R ELEVANT

T IMELY

So, what are some of these objectives?

1. Boost Brand Awareness

Digital marketing is all about boosting brand awareness. If your brand lacks the prevalence of behemoths like Google and Amazon, the first step in acquiring a new customer is achieving brand awareness.

Digital branding establishes your brand name in the customer's mind, grows your organic traffic, builds an online reputation, and increases faster conversation. Social media marketing, video marketing, and digital PR can boost brand awareness.

2. Boost Sales

The ultimate goal of a business is to boost its overall sales or leads. This is the driving force for achieving other business objectives.

The perfect marketing strategy should outline how sales can be increased, what channels and tactics you use, the budget required, and how to measure performance and results.

3. Reduced Cost

Companies or businesses running on a budget, reducing the overall customer acquisition cost, forms a viable objective. Various techniques like market automation, programmatic display advertising, and conversion rate optimization can reduce the cost.

4. Utilizing Digital Marketing to Generate Leads

A lead is a potential customer in your targeted audience who is interested in your brand or product. This is the first step in the digital marketing funnel and is achieved through marketing.

We can classify lead generation in digital marketing into three sets of marketing activities, namely:

- Generation of traffic to the business website

- Conversion of the website visitor into leads

- The conversation of the leads into customers

SEO, Google ads, Facebook ads and other tactics can be used to generate leads in digital marketing. Also, lead magnets, marketing automation techniques, and content can nurture leads further.

5. Grow Organic Search Traffic

The main challenge most businesses face is making sure that enough people are visiting their site or viewing their products and services, and not their competitors. Google SEO is one of the best methods to increase free organic traffic to your website, generate leads, and boost sales. SEO is the building block of digital marketing.

Consistent organic traffic on your blog or website, as a digital marketing objective, will create long-lasting online visibility and decrease the cost per customer acquisition.

1.3.2 Digital Marketing Strategies

Every business requires a marketing plan or strategy. Digital marketing strategy or plan is a blueprint that contains all the relevant information about your digital marketing objectives, product or services, your targeted audience, recent market trends, techniques, and channels used.

Here's how to build a simple marketing strategy:

- Outline marketing goals

- Outline customer profiles

- Identify your targeted audience

- Align ultimate business objectives with marketing goals

- Define the budget

- Determine the method of measuring results

- Review and re-test campaign performance

- Identify digital marketing techniques and channels

A well-crafted digital marketing strategy might help track your overall business goals, optimize your digital marketing results, and concentrate on your objectives.

Developing a Website for Digital Marketing

A website is an important aspect of digital marketing because all digital marketing elements direct traffic to a website. Digital marketing will only work and deliver results when your website is aligned with your digital marketing and company objectives.

A perfect website needs to be optimized for search engines to attract organic traffic from Google search. If the website lacks an effective SEO, it will not organically appear in the top on the Search Engine Result Page (SERP); therefore, it won't generate enough clicks from search engines. Clicks are very important to your digital marketing campaign because you require them to drive as much traffic as possible to your site and boost direct sales.

Setting up social media analytics and Google Analytics can help you measure your website traffic and capture information on how guests interact with your website and brand. To improve your search visibility and attract organic traffic, you can create a blog on your domain.

Search Engine Optimization (SEO)

SEO plays a critical role in how digital marketing works for businesses. Effective SEO allows your website to rank first on Google. Optimizing your website can bring unlimited organic traffic to your website and increase ROI efficiently than other digital marketing techniques.

Even though Google algorithms can be confusing sometimes; you'll understand it better while you are working with it. Google frequently makes changes to its algorithms, which affects SEO results.

One recent change involved the new HTTPS requirements. Google requires users who are using HTTP pages to switch to HTTPS format because most of the HTTP contact forms were not secure enough.

So, those websites that didn't change their HTTP to HTTPS designation lost their rank or placement on Google search engines.

1.3.3 Does Digital Marketing Work?

Digital marketing is now the most vital component of many

business strategies. Today, small businesses have access to cheap and efficient methods of promoting their products and services.

The digital market isn't limited by boundaries; it serves big, middle, and small businesses.

Using digital devices such as smartphones, laptops, tablets, smart TVs, billboards, social media, videos, games, e-mail, content, and many others, a company can now promote its brand, product, and service. Digital marketing is efficient than other forms of marketing because its top priority is to meet the needs and desires of users.

Companies are now using an integrated multi-channel marketing approach that combines all the elements of digital marketing to create an innovative customer experience. Through coordinating the company's marketing message across various digital platforms and using different tactics to support each marketing campaign, companies can create a unified brand message and boost the success of every digital marketing campaign.

Just like other forms of marketing that have to undergo trial and error, sometimes digital marketing falls short of meeting the company's marketing objectives. This doesn't make it imperfect, because it has revolutionized marketing in unthinkable ways.

Sample Case

How Miss Chase Used Sponsored ads and Stored to Create Strong Brand Presence

In the World of unique fashion designs, Miss Chase identifies its place as an apparel name that's high quality and always on-trend.

The Challenge

With so many competitors in the market, Miss Chase needed to create brand awareness and reach customers and get them to try its products and to understand how their quality differs from their competitors.

Lots of effort and love goes into creating each of Miss Chase products. Therefore, it's only fair for the brand to ensure that every product they launch is instantly promoted on Amazon to drive more sales.

The Solution

To achieve these goals, Miss Chase utilized a lot of Amazons Advertising products like a Store and sponsored ads. Miss chase ran both manual and automatic campaigns concurrently, tweaking bids and keywords, and inserting new keyword to existing promotions and tracking them constantly.

After a month of running the test to try to identify the perfect inputs for a successful promotion, Miss Chase switched using only manual campaigns. The brand created a robust strategy with unique ad groups with different types of targeting for each product line. When one of utilizing sponsored products elapsed, Miss Chase began using Store and sponsored brands to drive loyalty and awareness.

The Results

Miss Chase has increased its campaigns rapidly from 3 to 20 with over 4000 products advertised.

The combined effects of stores, sponsored products, and brands resulted in a spike in Miss Chase sales by 107%, since November 2018, with a return on investment of 370%. Roughly 30 percent of their total sales can be accredited to Amazon Advertising powers.

Our Take

◆ The future of marketing is digital marketing. If you haven't embraced it yet, now it's time to do so. Apart from the benefits that we have talked about, you can track the success of your digital marketing campaigns' efforts incredibly fast and accurately.

◆ With digital marketing, it's easy to see which marketing strategies are creating profits and which ones require more work.

◆ Now that you understand what digital marketing is, how it works, and why it's essential to your business, your next step is to start planning for your next digital marketing campaign.

◆ In our next chapter, we provide you with different digital marketing tactics, so you can effectively create and integrate your marketing strategies to drive sales and grow your business.

Quiz 1

1. **What's the right sequence of levels in the marketing funnel?**

    a. MOFU, TOFU, BOFU

    b. TOFU, MOFU, BOFU

    c. BOFU, MOFU, TUFU

    d. TOFU, BOFU, MOFU

2. **_____ is a stage where targeted prospects are already part of the marketing funnel, but still they haven't decided on purchasing the products.**

    a. Top of the Funnel (TOFU)

    b. Middle of the Funnel (MOFU)

    c. Bottom of the Funnel (BOFU)

3. **Consistent _____ on your website, as a digital marketing objective, will create long-lasting online visibility and decrease the cost per acquisition.**

    a. Facebook ads

    b. Google ads

    c. Organic traffic

    d. Lead Magnets

4. **We can classify lead generation in digital marketing as three sets of marketing activities which one is not?**

   a. Conversion of traffic to a business

   b. Conversion of the websites visitor into leads

   c. Conversion of leads into customer

   d. Conversion of prospects into influencers

5. **All the four Ps are important in digital marketing, which P, is digital marketing more dependent on?**

   a. Price

   b. Product

   c. Promotion

   d. Place

6. **What is the true difference between traditional and digital marketing?**

   a. Digital Marketing is efficient for lead generation and sales

   b. Digital and traditional marketing have the same efficiency

   c. Traditional marketing can be a better approach to boost sales and ROI

7. **Because of the rapid Growth of Search Engine Optimization, SEO marketing needs to be an aspect of your digital strategy.**

    a. Yes, it's should be the primary aspect

    b. Yes, it should be in the digital strategy, but it's not that important

    c. Yes, it all depends on the company's goals and objectives

8. **Which of the one is the odd one out?**

    a. Digital Advertisements

    b. Billboards

    c. Blogging

    d. Search Engine Optimization

9. **_____ is the process of executing and planning the pricing, promotion, distribution of goods and service, and idea to create an exchange that satisfies the individual, and organization objectives.**

    a. Search Engine Optimization

    b. Digital Strategies

    c. Marketing

    d. Cost Per Mile

10. **An organization isn't sure if digital marketing will work for them. Which of the following questions will help them make sound decisions?**

   a. Are their staff present on the internet?

   b. Are their prospects, influencers, and customers on the internet?

   c. Are they receiving any leads and sales from their current method of marketing?

   d. Are their competitors using digital marketing?

Solutions to the above questions can be downloaded from
the **Online Resources** *section of this book on*
www.vibrantpublishers.com

Chapter 2

Creating a Content Marketing Framework: Turning Prospect Visitors into Customers

The popularity of content marketing has grown exponentially over the past decade. Now, nearly all businesses and industries, regardless of their size, have understood the importance of creating content that makes the targeted audience more willing to engage and receptive to becoming customers.

However, the problem is that most companies usually take the unstructured approach when creating and marketing their digital content. According to a report by Smart Insight, about half of the digital marketers lack a content marketing strategy; instead, they prefer guessing which topics readers might be attracted to.

Filled with eagerness, these digital markets try to find and create attractive content that appeals to the targeted audience and persuade them to buy their products. As soon as they publish the content, these marketers sit and wait for potential customers to publish the content, these marketers sit and wait for potential customers to come pounding on their doors. Sadly, this never happens, their website never receives organic traffic, and sales never occur.

What they lack is a strategy. A structural way of creating, disseminating, and promoting all that valuable content they are creating. An effective content marketing strategy begins with a comprehensive understanding of what the targeted audience wants. What motivates them? What inspires them?

Once you understand these issues, you can shape and address your sales pitch with content developed around the analysis of the needs and desires of the targeted audience.

In this chapter, we will cover:

- How to perfectly create content marketing strategies for your business

- The techniques for creating a perfect content marketing strategy

- The different marketing funnels

- Metrics to measure content marketing strategies

2.1 Techniques of Well-Developed Content Marketing

Content marketing strategy involves the creation and distribution of relevant and valuable educational or compelling content on multiple formats to attract and retain customers and drive more organic leads to your site.

To achieve perfect content marketing, you have to first understand how the creation of unique and attractive content influences your overall digital marketing strategy.

When done right, content marketing will not only attract potential leads into your digital marketing funnel, but it will nurture those leads through the marketing funnel until they're converted into new customers and boost the overall growth of your business.

No! Content development is not all about blogging. This is just a big misconception. Even though blogs are a major part of content marketing, they are only one ingredient of the portion. When you dive deeper into this chapter, you will understand why blogs are not the most lucrative form of content marketing.

Let's look at some features of a complete marketing strategy.

2.1.1 Complete Content Marketing Comprises a Full Marketing Funnel

To convert a prospective visitor into a customer, he/she must undergo three stages:

1. Awareness

First, the potential visitor must realize a problem, and that you or your organization have a solution for it. Blogs excel in this stage because they inform the visitor of your solution.

2. Evaluation/Engagement

At this stage, prospects test the choice made available to them, either by you or your competitors, but at the end of the day, the prospect takes no initiative of solving the problem.

3. Conversion/Loyalty

Potential visitors or prospects that move to this stage are ready to make a purchase. It's your role as a digital marketer in this stage to convert visitors into customers.

A new prospect will never evaluate your solution if he/she isn't aware of the problem and the solution you're offering. Converting them into a customer will be impossible if they haven't evaluated the existing choices.

As a digital content marketer, you need to design specific content that meets the needs of prospects at every stage. This is the only way you can move a potential visitor through the marketing funnel.

To make this sound much easier…

Figure 2.1

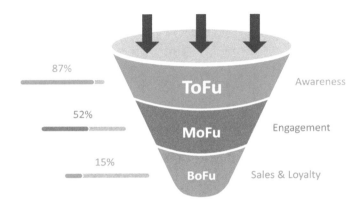

- The right content at the Top-of–the-Funnel will facilitate awareness.

- The right content in the Middle-of-the-Funnel will expedite the evaluation

- Finally, the right content at the Bottom- of-the-Funnel will lead to conversion.

1. Top of the Funnel Content Marketing

Once your targeted visitors enter the top of the marketing funnel, they are innocent; they don't know what their problem is.

It's your job to provide content that doesn't restrict the entry of the prospect into this stage. Because they have little to no motivation to peruse a problem, the content at the top of the funnel should be freely available, entertaining, educational, and inspiring enough.

Use readily available forms of content, like:

- Blog posts
- Infographics
- Photographs
- Podcasts
- e-Magazines
- Social Media Updates

You don't need all this at the top of the funnel.

Many businesses only use blogs and social media platforms to post their content. Blogs are very convenient at facilitating awareness, but they're poor at expediting evaluation and conversion. All the stages are important for your business, but the importance of evaluation and conversion stages surpass the awareness stage. Once you have understood how these two work, you can incorporate other forms of content like e-magazines, podcasts, etc.

It's the role of the digital marketer to understand that the goal of the content in this stage is to make potential visitors aware of their problem and the availability of a solution. Sadly, most businesses start and end their content marketing campaign at the top-of-the-funnel stage.

To be a smart content marketer, you need to put in more effort, so you can move your prospect from the awareness stage to the evaluation stage in the middle of the funnel. To ensure your prospect moves through the middle and bottom funnels, you'll require other types of content.

2. Middle of the Funnel Content Marketing

In this section, prospects are aware of the existing problem and solution. You now need to convert them into leads. The content used here encourages prospects to submit their contact information to receive future marketing content.

The content used in the middle of the funnel is known as the Lead Magnet, and it includes:

- Software downloads

- Surveys

- Webinars

- Educational resources

Quizzes are lead magnets that businesses can use to increase their lead captures rate. Many companies are receiving positive results for using quizzes as a type of lead magnet.

3. Bottom of the Funnel Content Marketing

The content used here aims to convert leads to customers. It should help your new lead make informed purchasing decisions.

Content in this stage includes:

- Events/webinars

- Mini-classes

- Comparisons

- Free trial

- Customer stories/reviews

Even though your leads might read your social media posts

or blogs and download your lead magnets, you still need to help them decide between you and your competitor before they buy a product.

Cloud margin customer stories or reviews prove that the company can handle the needs of its leads. Customer stories are assets that convert leads into customers. Usually, they're the liability assignment of the content marketing team.

As you can see, it's essential to have a blog at the top of the funnel, but if you fail to optimize your full digital marketing funnel, you won't be able to make any sales.

2.1.2 Create Intent-Based Content

For content marketing, intent means everything. What does the content aim to achieve? Is it to capture the attention of the reader? Do you want to inform a prospect of a new product available in the market?

You need to understand that all the content you create has a role, and it should be effective. A marketer needs to comprehend present intent, foresee future intent, and then develop content that addresses the intent every day.

The fact is, the most productive content resources you can create are those resources that meet the intent of the lead in the middle and bottom of the funnel. Not only does it capture new customers but keeps on returning the existing ones.

It is, therefore, crucial to work on the intent at the bottom and the middle of the digital marketing funnel before you can start creating expensive and time-consuming blogs for awareness at the top of the funnel.

Again, this doesn't diminish the value of blogs; it only ensures that you understand that to win in content marketing, higher priority should go to the middle and bottom digital marketing funnels.

2.1.3 Complete Content Marketing is Ascension Focused

The main goal of content marketing is to get leads and convert them, and you won't achieve that by nudging them throughout the digital marketing funnel.

Ascension here describes moving from one stage to another. Perfect content will make the ascension process as easy as possible for the prospective client. The easier the ascension process, the easier for the prospect to reach the bottom of the funnel.

You can integrate ascension offers like the one below into your assets. If prospects click the banner they will be taken to your landing page, where they can enter their content details and ascend into leads.

Figure 2.2

2.1.4 Complete Marketing Is Segmented

One of the common mistakes marketers make is trying to achieve too much while doing too little. Give each content resource one or two goals and concentrate on achieving the goals. Trying to cover too much in one content will destroy your credibility and bamboozle the prospects.

2.1.5 Complete Content Marketing is Cross Channeled

It's quite common to see the same content over multiple platforms. You can change your content on your blogs and post them on social media accounts (Twitter, Facebook, Pinterest, etc.).

Figuring out the best way to tweak your content to fit other platforms can help you reach a large audience without having to create any other additional content.

There are endless ways you can convert that attractive blog content to maximize exposure. You can expand it into an online class or webinar or make it into a podcast. Regardless of the method you choose, creating cross-channel content is the best way to go about with content marketing.

2.1.6 Complete Content Marketing Is Based on Avatars

As a digital marketer, your content should be able to satisfy the needs or the intent of the prospect avatar. You can target one avatar (*target marketing*) or multiple avatars.

2.2 Smart Content Development Tool

Creating, publishing, managing, and measuring your content success can be much easier with the right set of tools. The right tools will help you scale your development strategy and boost your business.

1. Content Management System (CMS)

A content management system allows easy creation, editing, management, and tracking of the success of your content on your site, whether it's a blog post, site page, e-mail campaign, or landing page.

A CMS removes the technical skills and design elements required to upload content to a website. As a marketer, you can write, optimize, and track all your content in one central place.

2. Customer Relationship Management (CRM) System

A customer relationship system allows you to store all the captured information when prospects fill in their contact information and convert. Without effective CRM, you or your marketing team can't organize customer contacts, qualify leads, and even raise a prospect into a sale.

3. Marketing Automation Software

Marketing automation software allows you to automate specific marketing activities. For example, you can automate your e-mail activities by activating certain e-mail nurture campaigns based on the behavior of visitors' actions on your site. As your business expands, this tool might be the key to stretch your assets and utilize your marketing resources fully.

4. Analytics Tools

A marketer should always follow up on their content. By using data analytics to insert keywords into your content, you can attract the right traffic to your website, see which content ranks higher based on engagement levels, and determine which content offers lots of leads. With the data collected, you can optimize your existing content and develop better and more efficient content.

2.3 Content Marketing Plan

Your content marketing strategy will only be successful if you have a plan.

A content marketing plan should include:

1. Marketing Funnel
Contain all the three marketing funnels–TOFU, MOFU, and BOFU.

2. Avatar
The prospects your content targets.

3. Content Type
Is it an audio, video, blog, or e-mail?

4. Channels
Where will you post your content?

5. **Call-To-Action/Ascension Path**
   What CTA are you going to use for your content?

2.4 Tactics to Measure Content Marketing Success

You can measure your content marketing success by using the following tactics:

Traffic by Channel

Measure traffic from the top of the funnel stage using multiple social media channels like Twitter, Facebook, LinkedIn, Pinterest, YouTube, and Google.

Net New Marketing-Qualified Leads (MQLs)

You can measure the leads being created in the middle of the funnel to determine how much information needs to be added before they are ready to make a purchase.

Conversion Rate

Perfect content marketing creates traffic to product pages and leads forms. To measure the success of your strategy, measure the conversion rate on your product pages, lead forms, and other forms of CTA.

Net New Sales- Qualified Leads(SQLs)

Determine the leads expanding content at the bottom of the funnel. This shows they're ready to purchase your product or brand.

Our Take

◆ Content marketing is crucial for any company or business that wants to grow their leads and sales in today's digital world.

◆ Content marketing isn't about blogging alone. A blog is just one of the many channels you can use in your content marketing campaigns.

◆ With the help of the above conversation, you will have the best starting point for creating your complete content marketing strategy.

Quiz 2

1. **Three of the following are features of a complete marketing strategy. Which one is the odd one out?**

   a. Awareness

   b. Conversion

   c. Solution

   d. Engagement

2. **Top of the funnel content marketing....................**

   a. Expedite evaluation

   b. Facilitate awareness

   c. Lead to conversion

3. **Which one of the following best describes the content management system?**

   a. allows you to store all the captured information when prospects fill in their contact information and convert

   b. allows easy creation, editing, management, and tracking of the success of your content on your site, whether it's a blog post, site page, e-mail campaign, or landing page.

   c. allows you to automate specific marketing activities.

4. The main goal of ……………….. is to get leads and convert them, and you won't achieve that by nudging them throughout the digital marketing funnel.

    a. A Digital marketer

    b. Content marketing

    c. Content creation

    d. Funneling

5. The bottom of the funnel content marketing is achieved through three of the following four ways. Which one is not?

    a. Free trial

    b. Comparisons

    c. Webinars

    d. Podcasts

6. What does a Content Management System do?

    a. Allows the automation of specific marketing activities.

    b. Allows the creation, editing, management, and tracking of content on a website.

    c. It allows marketers to insert specific keywords into their content to attract the right traffic to their website.

7. **Ways of measuring content marketing success entail the following except?**

   a. Traffic by channel

   b. Conversion rate

   c. Net new sales-qualified leads (SQLs)

   d. Content-type

8. **When done right, _____will not only attract potential leads into your digital marketing funnel, but it will nurture those leads through the marketing funnel until they're converted into new customers and boost the overall growth of your business.**

   a. Content marketing

   b. Blogging

   c. Digital marketing

   d. Content development

9. **The following are components of a Content Marketing Plan, which one is not**

   a. Marketing

   b. Avatar

   c. Analytic tools

   d. Channels

   e. Call –to-Action

10. Content marketing is_____

    a. Intent-based

    b. Credible

    c. Complete

Solutions to the above questions can be downloaded from
the **Online Resources** *section of this book on*
www.vibrantpublishers.com

This page is intentionally left blank

Chapter 3

Digital Advertising: Creating A Plan That Works

D igital advertising is the major element of today's marketing structures, and if it's not part of your business strategy, it should be. Regardless of your business size or type, digital advertising, will help you to successfully grow your online presence and eventually nurture more conversion and sales.

The adaptation of digital advertisement allows your organization to have more prominence throughout a much wider audience. It's therefore important to craft a strategic digital marketing advertising campaign that will not only reach your targeted audience but also increase your ROI significantly.

However, if your ads are not well structured, you won't achieve the results you were hoping for. Digital advertising has a lot of moving parts, and each part must be taken into consideration for it to work in your favor.

In this chapter, you will receive an overview of how to plan, set up, and optimize your ad campaign for your business, including the necessary metrics for measuring the ad campaign's performance.

In this chapter, we will learn:

- What a Digital Advertising Plan is.

- The difference between organic and inorganic traffic.

- How to Implement Digital Advertising Easily

- Components of a Digital Advertising Plan.

- Developing an Ad Campaign

- The Metrics

What's a Digital Advertising Plan?

To understand what a digital advertising plan is, we must first understand what digital advertising is.

Digital advertising is the process of delivering various forms of marketing information to various users online via digital channels. It takes advantage of mediums like mobile apps, websites, search engines, affiliate programs, and social media to display ads and marketing messages to prospects.

Digital advertising is heavily data driven, meaning it can give you information on your campaigns and results in a matter of minutes. Its ability to use data and target certain groups makes it a crucial tool for businesses and organizations to connect with their audience.

3.1 A Little Overview of Paid Traffic

While being connected to the world offers your endless means of reaching out to your audiences and engaging them, there is a line that differentiates organic "free" and inorganic "paid." Digital marketing is an inorganic method to reach and communicate with your audience.

Paid traffic is a very powerful marketing tool that grants small and medium businesses direction and control over their marketing efforts. Technically, paid traffic comes from any service you pay to drive traffic to your site, be it Facebook or paid search (Bing Ads and Google AdWords).

The Benefits of Paid Traffic

1. You can choose exactly what you want to spend to drivpaid traffic to your website.

2. Easily set the amount you wish to spend on the various forms of advertising (PPC).

3. Keyword optimization allows you to strategically drive your targeted audience to your website.

Drawbacks of Paid Traffic

Just because a visitor has clicked your link at the top of their google search and visited your site, it doesn't mean they will like what you are selling or providing. You are receiving more prospects to your site but they are under no obligation to buy your products. As a result, paid traffic doesn't necessarily increase your conversion rate or sales.

A poorly designed website coupled up with high traffic is a remedy for disaster. If your visitors leave your site as soon as they enter, your bounce rate will increase. A higher bounce rate will result in your website being ranked lower in Google. To make the matter worse, you're still paying for the page visits.

3.1.1 Best Sources for Paid Traffic

According to Business Insider, Google site and Facebook generate over 80% referral traffic. That's more than the combined traffic of other sites.

1. Google

Google is the most preferred search engine and most people turn to it whenever they encounter a problem and want to find a solution or more information on the problem. Google is considered one of the best paid-traffic creators, and it will help you boost visitor engagements and brand awareness.

Google uses specific keywords to target various audiences with specific interests. You will be in control of your cost if you set the daily maximums, measurements, and manage your ad campaign via quantitative analysis.

2. Facebook

People turn to Facebook for entertainment. On the Facebook newsfeed, users get to see comments, promoted posts, and ads.

If you are willing to part with a few dollars for your business, you too can also get your ads displayed on the newsfeed of your targeted audience. You don't have to spend so much to expand your reach.

Facebook being a social media platform collects data on their users' behaviors every day, so they know what the users prefer the most. This makes them one of the most convenient ad platforms in the world today.

Facebook ad campaigns are so effective at promoting awareness and increasing traffic to your website because with it, you can precisely target the behavior, geographic location, and demographic of your audience.

3. YouTube

Being the second-largest search engine in the world, people rely on it for a wide range of services. Whether that is vlogs, the latest music, movie trailers, educational content, and more! There is a lot of traffic from YouTube, and the fun part is it's cheap. You can use the normal banner ads or run video ads or use both concurrently on YouTube—it all depends on your preferences.

If you have some quality video content, YouTube is the place to be. Because it tracks users' frequency on specific videos, what they like, and the channels they like, you can precisely target your prospects.

3.2 How to Implement Digital Advertising Easily

Here we look into how you can create advertisements that attract your prospects.

3.2.1. Concepts of Evaluating Your Target Audience

To evaluate your targeted audience, use the two concepts below:

The Customer Journey

The customer journey is a complete experience of the customer's interaction with a business. It comprises all the encounters throughout every stage of a customer life cycle from awareness to loyalty.

Figure 3.1

The journey can be divided into three important stages:

1. Awareness

In the early stages of a customer's journey, he might not be aware that your product exists or even aware of the problem. The awareness stage exists to not only expose your brand to your customers but to touch pain points that your product might remedy.

2. Evaluation

In this phase, prospects are evaluating whether to address the problem or not. Interested individuals are most likely to research more on your brand, but let's face it—the competition out there is fierce. It all boils down to how you stack up.

3. Conversion

Here, potential customers have decided that they're ready to purchase your product.

State of Traffic/Traffic Temperature

The state of traffic is the way we classify different sources of traffic and the associations marketers have with prospects from the various sources.

Cold Traffic: People who have never heard of your brand.

Warm Traffic: Audiences that have made some kind of connection with your brand or product, they have clicked your ads, and have shown interest in what you're offering. We can refer to these people as acquaintances who have yet to be converted into customers.

Hot Traffic: These are leads who have purchased your products.

The main aim of a digital marketer is to move the audience from cold to hot, changing new visitors to committed customers who are willing to purchase your product repeatedly.

The message of your ad campaign should match the prospect temperature.

In cold traffic, you don't have so much control, so you should aim to build an association with your prospects, while in hot traffic your relationship is built. These different states or temperatures describe various kinds of audiences. This correlates with the stages which we mentioned earlier.

If you have figured out the three audience segments, now you need to understand the specific goals of your traffic campaign. Is It ...

Indoctrination: Introducing your brand in the market for the people who have never heard about it.

Acquisition: Converting leads.

Monetization: Selling your best product or service to the best and repeated customer.

All your campaigns will have a different goal and will produce different results. So, it's vital to evaluate the entire process and calculate what you're going to spend vs. profit. Usually, you will lose money with an indoctrination campaign, break even with an acquisition campaign, and make profits with a monetization campaign.

3.3 Five Elements of High Performing Advertisement Campaigns

1. The Offer

An offer here isn't the same as your product or service, but a combination of the two with an addition of other bonuses or add-ons, including all your promotion details, such as the price, deliverables, scheduling, and others.

Your business might be providing one product or service, but you can offer it for sale in various ways, resulting in hundreds of different offers.

A business offer is the starting point of an ad campaign. Usually, if you get it right, then the rest will fall in place on its own. But if you fail, everything will fall apart.

2. Ad Copy

An ad copy refers to the information used in the campaign ad. It should be clear and convincing, outlining the benefits of engaging the ad. A good ad copy is persuasive and intriguing without the hype—has an emotional hook to it.

You want to start your ad copy by concentrating on the problem your targeted audience is facing, then offer a solution to the problem. If people relate to the problem, then they'll be eager to learn about the solution you are offering.

3. The Creative

The creativity of your ad is important—don't exaggerate it. The images, carousel images, or videos should convey the message visually in a matter of seconds. This way, it can support and enhance your ad copy.

Apple's creative drove over eight million impressions in roughly six weeks by creating an intriguing and concise AirPods creative, which ultimately drove the consumers to purchase their product.

The design of your ad should go hand in hand with the brand's message. If you create a strong representation of your brand, it will do the talking for you.

4. Ad Consistency

Your ad needs to be seamless throughout your campaign.

This is important because it relays the element of trust, which is a factor of conversion. If a person feels that your offer is real, he/she will consider your offer. Create a sense of fear or doubt and see how fast they'll exit without a second glance.

Your visitors should always feel like they are on a safe path and not feel like they are being duped.

The only way to achieve this is by being consistent—visually, in your ad message, and the demonstration of your offer—from your ad to your landing page, or any other campaign piece.

Consistency depends on three elements, namely:

- Design: Use the same colors and images on each piece of your campaign.

- Messaging: Utilize the same catchphrases and benefits in your ad and also on the landing page.

- Offer: Your landing pages and campaign levels should feature the safe offer. Also, repeat it at your thank-you page and follow-up e-mail too.

Ad consistency is paramount in your digital advertising campaign. It will not only boost your conversion rate but also lower your costs.

5. Targeting

Targeting is the final element in the ad campaign, and it's very important because even a perfect offer won't convert if placed in front of the wrong audience.

There only two rules when planning your targeting:

- **Be as specific as possible**
  Do in-depth research on the audience you're targeting. The objective here is to learn everything about your targeted audience until you can exactly pinpoint the interests that make them different from other groups.

- **Get the right message to your prospects at any temperature.**
  Every message should correlate with the relationship you have with your targeted audience at each state/temperature.

Cold Traffic

With cold traffic, you are just introducing yourself to the target audience, so you have only three goals:

1. **Indoctrination:** Building credibility and trust by freely sharing valuable information.

2. **Retargeting:** Once your content attracts attention, pixel (*adding a code to your website to track conversions from your ads*) them so you can run more ads to them; warming them up.

3. **Segmentation**: If they click on your content, then they are interested in what you have to say; you can offer more relevant content later.

Examples of offers you make to cold traffic:

- Social media updates

- Blog posts

- Lead magnets

- White papers

- Podcasts

- Quiz/Survey

Warm Traffic

Warm traffic consists of acquaintances interested in your business, but that haven't made a purchase—yet! They have visited one or two of your social media platforms. Nevertheless, they have interacted with you, but not taken the step. Target your ads here to:

- Leads that joined your e-mail list

- To the website visitors who have been pixelated

- Social media subscribers.

The goal here is to:

- Generate leads

- Drive low-ticket sales

Warm traffic offers you could make to your targeted customers

- Free webinars

- Flash sales

- Product Demos

- Books

- Software

- Free trials

- Low-dollar offers

Hot Traffic

These are the buyers. Who doesn't love the buyers?

This group knows all about you, and they have purchased from you. But you can't just abandon them! You want them to come back again and again. When you deploy ads and e-mail marketing campaigns, you're ensuring your hot audience doesn't forget about you.

The goals of hot traffic are:

- High-dollar sales

- Activation

Hot-traffic offers for your targeted audience:

- Paid Webinars

- High-dollar offers

- Events

- Just for you services

Getting the temperature right allows you to precisely target your ads.

Developing an Ad Campaign

In this section, we are going to see how we can use all these elements and concepts to develop a converting ad campaign.

The secret is to develop everything in advance (copy, creative, and targeting) before trying to work on a campaign. The goal here is to create precisely targeted ads that appeal to the targeted audience, and what better way than using the **Ad Grid**.

Ad Grid

The ad grid is a perfect system for creating campaigns that align perfectly with the interests and temperature of your targeted audience.

The concept behind the ad grid is identifying your targeted audience in advance and what might attract them, so you can be sure of what to include on your campaign message. Develop your ad grid on Excel or Google Sheet.

3.4 How to Implement and Scale Your Ad Campaign

1. Identify Your Avatars

An avatar is a profile of the person you are targeting. Identify at least 3-4 different avatars for each of your traffic campaigns.

To find the best avatars, take a look at your offer and try to figure out several different types of people who might want it and benefit from it.

The people you'll select will be an avatar for your campaign. Enter them into the top of your ad grid spreadsheet.

2. Determine the Interests

What makes your offer so interesting? Each advantage of your offer can be converted into a point of interest to gain the attention of your audience.

We can categories the interests based on five questions:

- What will they have when they consume your offer? How will it affect their life afterward?

- How will they feel after accepting an offer? (i.e., smarter, better, or more successful?)

- What effect did you have on their average lives?

- What proof do you have that validates your offer?

- Talk about the time-saving and quickness of applying the information in your offer.

Once you have the points of interest, input that on the first column of your ad grid.

3. Develop Your Ad Copy

Create different messages for each cell in your spreadsheet, each targeting a specific interest and avatar.

Each segment should have a unique ad copy. Avatar 1/Interest 1, Avatar 2/Interest 2, etc. Also, for each segment, the text of the entire ad copy should appear like text, headline, description, and type of ad.

So, if you have three avatars and three interests, then you'll need nine ads.

This kind of detail increases your chance of a successful campaign. Instead of creating ads that try to appeal to anyone, you'll create refined and targeted advertising specifically for your desired audience.

4. Avatar Research

Now that you are done writing your copy, you need to research your avatars to identify which interest groups you will use to make the ads.

Research each avatar separately to find answers to the following questions:

- Who are the big brands, thought leaders, or authority in your niche?

- What newspapers, books, or magazines does your potential customer read?

- What kind of events do your avatars participate in?

- Which website do they visit frequently?

- Where are they from?

- What unique feature is in this group?

You can search for the answers by doing a Google search or you can ask people in your targeted audience. This process might take time, but it's worth it because the answers to these questions will help you get your ads to your ideal people.

5. Develop Ad Creatives

Develop unique creatives for each interest. Go to Google and search for the point of interest and check out the results. The images that rank higher will give you an overview of what people think about when they hear of your keyword.

Take the top images as your inspiration and come up with a unique creative that is associated with your keyword. Incorporate the brand's unique look and feel.

6. Set Up Your Ads and Gather Your Results

Now that you have all the assets needed for the marketing campaigns, set up your ad. Use an ad planner, build each ad.

- Utilize the avatar for the targeting
- Use the ad copy and creative to develop your ads
- Based on the avatar interest, create an audience size ranging from half a million to 1.5 million for each

Turn your ads on and then run them for a week. Once the results start flowing in, gather up your metrics for analysis.

Based on your campaign purpose and temperature of the targeted audience, your best metric might be:

- Cost per click
- Cost per acquisition
- ROI
- Conversion

Record the metric on your ad grid just below the ad copy for each avatar/interest.

7. Scale-Up

To scale up means finding out what is working, what isn't working, and what needs to be done for better outcomes.

Two Methods of Scaling Up a Campaign

Horizontally: If one of your avatars receives more than average results, buy traffic on other ad platforms to increase your visibility to that specific audience.

Vertically: If a certain point of interest is very successful, develop more ads to that group of interest on the same platform.
Find your winning avatars and points of interest and scale them. Also refine your process to get better results within the shortest time, with fewer costs.

Optimizing an Ad Campaign

If your digital advertising campaign isn't performing well, take a look at your offer. If your offer is perfect, chances are other elements of your ad might be weak. But if your offer is all wrong, there's no chance that you can convert.

Your ad might start strong, but deteriorate with time, meaning that it has been viewed by too many people. To fix this, retarget the ad to another group of people or change the ad campaign completely.

3.5 Metrics to Measure Your Digital Advertising Campaign

Here are some major metrics to pay attention to as a digital advertiser.

Click-Through Rate (CTR)

CTR is the percentage of persons who clicked on your ad to persons who saw your ad. With this metric, you can check the effectiveness of your ad. Higher CTR means a more effective and significant ad.

Cost-Per-Lead (CPL)

CPL is the number of ads spent divided by the number of leads generated.

Cost-Per-Click (CPC)

CPC refers to how much your business pays, on average, for someone to click your ad.

Cost-Per-Acquisition (CPA)

CPA is the average cost of acquiring a new customer. It's calculated by dividing your total cost of the ad campaign by the number of conversions for gaining a new customer.

Cost-Per-Thousand (CPM)

Cost per thousand (mille) is how much your organization pays for 1,000 impressions of your ad. This is the metric to use when you are building a campaign to build awareness.

Sample Case

Babybel Drives Store Sales with smart targeting: YouTube Sample Case

The Challenge

Bel UK a company that sells Babybel snacks wanted to attract more audiences and drive more intent among people of all ages.

The company's chief goal was to increase its brand presence among pre-family adults (persons aged 25-34) and its core brand audience families with children.

The Solution

Showcasing its two famous products, the Babybel Light and Babybel original, the company's 'Super Snack" promotion advertised Babybel as the perfect all-round snack: rich in protein, convenient and natural. The message centered on the promotion crew; whose major mission is to save snack time when you feel famished.

The promotion comprised Video on demand, Social media, mobile, PR sampling, and YouTube.

The purpose of YouTube was to reach pre-family adults via targeting strategy customized for them. In the promotional creation, the team utilized YouTube Live Stages, demographic targeting, and affinity audiences: persons getting married, sports fans, or graduating.

The ten-second YouTube ad portrayed Super Snacks' main character in a real kitchen surrounding, as they addressed and directed the audience. The brand signature "Saving Snack Time" fortified the brand uniqueness.

The YouTube campaign ran back-to-back for two months. The first segment resulted in an impressive performance, with the snack achieving a 0.005 euros per view compared to 0.04 euros. Nevertheless, the promotion did not uplift the customers' intent.

To convince consumers to head to stores and purchase the snack, the promotion made a few changes to the creative portraying the characters delivering a CTA (Call to Action): "Select us whenever you feel famished, we are in the cheese lane!"

The Results

Because of the small tweak, the second segment resulted in half the cost per view of 0.005, along with an uplift in consumer purchase intent by 18% as compared to the company's 2.5% benchmark.

By the end of the promotion, the brand gained a lift of 70% in ad recall (compared to 23% benchmark) and a brand lift interest of 457%.

YouTube Adverts reached 4.67 million users. The company's great YouTube content also meets the company's expectation by successfully reaching the targeted audience, surpassing the sales target, and maintaining the company ahead of its competitors.

According to the Babybel team, 4 important factors helped in their YouTube success and eventually the influence of purchase intent of Grocery shoppers.

- Creating a memorable ad creative.

- Targeting the right audience

- Adding a clear and concise call to action to drive prospects to stores.

- Using YouTube's Brand Lift Study as a reliable source optimized truth ad.

Our Take

◆ Digital advertising is a vital component of Digital Marketing because it gives marketers a way to control the flow of traffic to their websites.

◆ However, for this to be successful, digital marketers need to curate various campaigns to target customers in every stage of the customer journey. Also, they need to understand the state of the traffic (temperature) in each stage. If you get these right, you will not only drive traffic to your site but also convert them to customers.

Quiz 3

1. Which one is not a metric to measure a company's Digital Advertising Campaign?

   a. CPM

   b. CPA

   c. CPV

   d. CPM

2. According to business insider Facebook and Google site generates what percentage of referral traffic?

   a. 100%

   b. 50%

   c. 80%

   d. 90%

3. The following are stages of the customer journey, which one is not?

   a. Evaluation

   b. Intent

   c. Awareness

   d. Conversion

4. **At what traffic temperature does the audience show interest in what the company is offering?**

   a. Cold Traffic

   b. Hot Traffic

   c. Warm Traffic

5. **A company wants to implement a digital advertising campaign which element would you suggest with?**

   a. The Creative

   b. An offer

   c. An Ad Copy

   d. Targeting

6. **_____ building credibility and trust by sharing valuable information for free.**

   a. Retargeting

   b. Segmentation

   c. Indoctrination

7. **Which statement better describes hot traffic?**

   a. Prospects that are interested in your product but haven't purchase anything.

   b. The audience that has been converted to long term customers.

   c. Visitors that are just showing interest in your product.

8. **Paid traffic is a powerful marketing tool that grants small and medium business direction and control over their marketing efforts. Which of the following is not a benefit of Paid Traffic?**

   a. Let's you choose what to spend to derive paid traffic to your site.

   b. Increases your website bounce rate.

   c. It allows you to easily set the amount of money you want to spend on various forms of advertising.

   d. It allows you to use keyword optimization to strategically drive your targeted audience to your website.

9. **Which statement is right about Digital Advertising?**

   a. It allows companies to use data to target certain groups of people.

   b. It takes advantage of mediums like mobile apps, websites, search engines, etc.

   c. It's highly data-driven therefore resulting in results in a matter of minutes.

   d. All the above

10. _____ is a perfect system for creating campaigns that align perfectly with the interests and temperature of your targeted audience.

    a. Ad copy

    b. Ad creatives

    c. Ad Grid

Solutions to the above questions can be downloaded from the **Online Resources** *section of this book on*
www.vibrantpublishers.com

This page is intentionally left blank

Chapter 4

Critical Components of Social Media Marketing

Social media platforms are where all customers interact with their brands. That being said, if you are not communicating directly to your customers through social media channels such as Instagram, Twitter, Pinterest, or Facebook, then you are missing out on a lot.

Superb social media marketing can generate devoted brand advocates, drive leads and sales, and result in remarkable success for your business.

Facebook remains one of the largest social media platforms in the world. In North America, 62.1 percent of people use Facebook, and the percentages for other places in the world are equally overwhelming.

It's like its own country now; the number of Facebook users exceeds the populations of most countries in the world.

Imagine that!

That's only Facebook. We haven't taken into account other

platforms.

Because of the widespread use of social media, more and more remarkable marketing opportunities are being created every day.

So, if you are not leveraging on the power of social media now, it's the time, or else you will lose in the long run.

This chapter will show you how to incorporate the components of social media marketing to achieve your desired outputs and maximize the impact on your bottom line.

In this chapter, we will learn:

- The key components that make up a perfect social media

- The importance of each component and how it affects your digital marketing campaigns

- The metrics to track the success of social media success

4.1 Key components of a perfect social media account

- Social Listening
- Social Influencing
- Social Networking
- Social Selling

Each of these keys is important at meeting different business objectives and the overall success of social media. But they all depend on the first component: Social Listening.

Social listening sheds the light on what you have to do in the other three parts. It will help you develop a social media marketing strategy that will give not only give you influence, but also a strong network and lots of sales.

Social listening aims to get your brand information in front of your prospects and customers. For many businesses, this means using one of the top social networking platforms (Facebook, Instagram, Twitter, Pinterest, and LinkedIn).

Don't worry that you will spend lots of time on social media sites, because you won't. Social media isn't about socializing with your prospects or customers—rather, it's about implementing the social cycle while reducing the costs.

The reality is that people use social media every day, and it's not only once a day, but multiple times.

4.1.1 Social Listening

Listen before you talk. It's something we were told growing up. For businesses, it's important to listen, because whether or not you are paying attention, people are talking about you and reaching out to you through your social media channels.

Customers might talk about how much they love your product, or they might try to reach out to you through your social media platforms for customer support requests.

Famous companies know how to use social media effectively. Take, for example, Nike, which has created a Twitter account dedicated to addressing customer service issues. Most times they respond to direct replies, but sometimes they can identify a trend and address it immediately.

Companies need to understand the importance of a strong reputation and following on social media. When your brand has gained a household name, then you have achieved brand awareness.

However, you don't want to be famous for all the wrong reasons. Scandals and bad services can cause negative social media reputation. If you receive positive comments, celebrate them, and send a thank-you response. If the comments are negative, take immediate action to address the problem and win the trust of your followers.

Because social media marketing can suddenly become a rocky adventure, it's important to continuously track your business and social media channels and look out for any problems. This is where social listening comes in.

Social listening involves monitoring your brand or product social media pages for mentions, customer feedback on your brands, and discussion on topics relating to your brand, business, or competitors. Also, there is the use of analysis to gather insights on opportunities and red flags.

Tracking of mentions and conversion is just one part of social listening—without analysis and responses, your brand cannot perfectly meet the needs of your visitors and customers.

Social listening is about coming up with a well-crafted response that not only provides real value, but also elicits brand loyalty and increases buyer retention rates.

Reasons to Use Social Listening

Customers want to be heard on social media platforms. They want businesses to respond to their questions and comments. Responding to your brand social media channels can make a huge difference. Customers are most likely going to buy from a brand that puts their needs first.

Here are the reasons for adopting social listening:

- Identify topics that spike interest in your followers

- Conduct customer research

- Track your brand growth

- Perform competitive research

- Track the influence of the industry to the people

- Increase customer acquisition

5 Things to Watch Out For

Brand: Track the mentioning of your brand name, the product or services you offer, or any other relevant information.

Topics relevant to your business: You always need to stay on top of the market in your area of specialization. So, listen to the topics your followers are talking about, their questions, and what makes them tick.

Competitors: Track what's being said about your competitors. Is it positive or negative? Also, track what your competitors are saying about you.

Influencers: Listen to the topics influencers and thought leaders are discussing and look at the content they are producing. They show where the market is heading.

Leaders Mentioning: Look for conversations mentioning your company leaders and influencers. See what people are saying. Is it good or bad?

Listening immerses you into your followers' world to see how they perceive your brand, your industry, and what topics are relating to your company. Also, it helps you identify the content and product challenges that need to be addressed.

Social Listening Tools You Can Use:

1. Awairio

2. Tweetdeck

3. Brandwatch

4. Hootsuite

5. Hubspot

Implementing Social Listening

Listening is effective, but there is more to social listening than being an avid social media listener. You need to know how to act on the things you hear and see.

You need a strategic "feedback loop." A feedback loop is not a scientific process; rather, it is a way for your marketing teams to address an issue that arises during social listening. It simply states out the departments or people that issues should be directed to and who resolves them.

How Does a Feedback Loop Work?

Companies put social listeners in place to actively listen. When an issue arises, a social listener will respond with an empathetic reply, then route the issue to the person in the team responsible for handling it.

All this happens within 12-24 hours of the complaint. Once the forwarded issue reaches a specialist, he/she will respond to the issue as quickly as possible. The respective teams or departments need to reply to the issue at hand so the issue doesn't get overlooked or forgotten, resulting in a bad brand reputation.

- Customer care teams should handle customer service complaints.

- Content teams should handle content complaints.

- Product teams should handle product complaints.

This way, the social media listener will know who to liaise with when an issue arises, facilitating a quick response.

Steps for Addressing Social Media Complaints

Social media marketing works only if you are authentic and human enough.

What do we mean by this?

When dealing with complaints, try to put yourself in the complainant's shoes and show compassion.

Here is how you can achieve this:

Respond Quickly: Social media is a quick platform; make sure you reply and address the complaints within 12-24 hours.

Empathize: Use empathic replies like, "I can understand how this upsets you" or "I know how frustrating this must be" where possible.

Move the Conversation: If you can't handle the issue in one or two sentences, shift the conversation to a private channel (the inbox) and remove from public eyes. Make a call, write a private message, or e-mail to the complainant to get detailed information about the issue.

With this approach, you will not only show that you are listening, but also that you're compassionate. By making the conversation private, it shows that you're committed to finding a solution to the problem.

Measures to Track Your Social Listening Efforts

Here are some metrics to watch:

1. **Content gaps identified:** This refers to identifying what content should be developed to tackle issues and questions before they arise.

2. **Refund rate:** Being able to fix issues without offering refunds.

3. **Reputation:** Are your customers happy or sad when talking to you and your products?

4. **Retention rate:** Are your customers staying or leaving?

5. **Product gaps identified:** What features or improvements are your followers and fans suggesting?

4.1.2 Social Influencing

Social influencing means exactly what you think—influencing the attitudes, behaviors, and attitudes of your followers. Since you have been listening to your followers, it will be relatively easy to influence them.

Because you already know what they are talking about and the topics they are interested in, the next is just to introduce your neutral, authoritative voice.

How will you know if your influence is growing?

- Increased follower engagements as more and more people are responding and sharing your posts.

- Increased traffic as more and more people visit your site.

- Becoming recognized as authority or brand

- Development of greater mind-share as people share their questions, opinions, and thoughts with you.

The success of this stage is influenced highly by social listening. Even at this stage, you will still be listening.

Objectives for Social Influencing

In this stage, you are trying to:

- Boost engagement with your content and products

- Start conversations relating to the topics around your business

- Increase website traffic

- Increase your product awareness

- Grow your re-targeting list

Metrics to Measure Your Social Influence

1. **Site engagement rates:** Check whether you are getting more social shares or comments.

2. **Re-targeting List Growth:** Re-targeting marketing helps to get your content to your targeted audience.

3. **Traffic by Channel:** Is your social media traffic increasing?

4. **Offer Awareness:** Followers see and respond to your offers in the various social media channels.

4.1.3 Social Networking

Figure 4.1

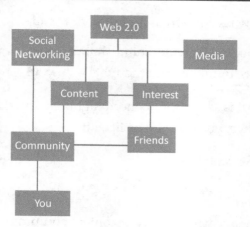

Social networking is essential to all businesses, big or small. Companies use social networking to boost brand visibility and encourage customer devotion through authorities and marketers.

Because it makes the company more visible to both new and existing customers, social networking helps marketers promote brand content and voice.

Social networking can cause a deep, long-lasting relationship with your followers and prospects and improve conversion rates.

Objectives of Social Networking

The aim of social networking is to:

- Distribute content that's meant to fill the gaps left by your content. It may target the same topic or something different.

- Create a good relationship with the brand offering the same products as yours.

- Maximize the relationship to develop profitable partnerships.

- Build a stronger brand, resulting in increased sales.

Metrics to Measure the Strength of Your Social Network

The Number of Inbound Links: With a strong network, your backlinks to your content will increase.

Description of Earned Media Mentions: Consider the number, relevance, and value of the mentions, and where they come from.

Explanation of Gained Calculated Partnerships: Have you reached out to prospects? How many are reaching back to you? And are the relationships valuable?

4.1.4 Social Selling

The final component in our list is social selling.

Social selling is using social media to find, connect, and convert leads. Today, social selling is the best way to develop meaningful relationships with your potential prospects so that when they think of buying a product, they think of your brand.

Social selling is not a quick one-time deal……

However, social media pla tforms are the primary territory for interacting with potential prospects and building rapport for new business connections.

You have listened to your prospects, built authority in your space, and established a strong social network, so now it's time to put your offer to your prospect and convert them to sales.

Apart from being about having access to contacts, it is also about building relationships and knowing the right time to enter conversations and offer your solution to a problem.

The aim is to address the problems your potential customer faces and make his/her life much easier, instead of being a nuisance online.

Why Your Business Should Care About Social Selling

- It allows your team to build relationships.

- Your top competitors are already using social selling.

- It keeps your clients engaged in social buying.

- Create leads to boost your e-mail list.

- Gain new customers and upsell existing customers.

- Grow buyer frequency by making them buy repeatedly.

Metrics to Track the Success of Social Selling

- **The Number of Visitors:** Is your number of leads growing?

- **Buyer Frequency:** Are your customers buying repeatedly?

- **Offer Conversion Rate:** Are you converting leads into a customer?

4.2 Social Media Success Metrics

Even though we have hinted about various metrics for tracking each of the four components of social marketing, few other metrics can highlight the overall direction of your social media marketing strategy.

Traffic by Channel

You can measure your traffic by channel by using tools like BuzzSumo and others. This way, you can know where your traffic is coming from. Increased engagement means that your topic resonates with your targeted audience. Low engagement means your topic needs improvements.

Direct Response Metrics

Measure how your customers and followers react to the content you post and share, because it is important for any marketing strategy. These metrics help you to figure out whether your targeted audience shows interest in what you're publishing and inform you of the content type you should post in the future.

Conversion from Social Media

You know the traffic that's coming from social media channels, now you need to know how to calculate how many leads are being converted.

To find the conversion rate for social media, divide traffic from social media with the total traffic. The value you get is the number of visits you want to impact. If your conversion rate is higher, your social media marketing is successful.

Monitor Motions

Your audience is talking about you continuously, and you need to be part of the conversations. Tracking your mentions in essential, and you achieve this by activating notifications on your social media accounts. If your followers aren't tagging you, use a third-party tool to track mentions on Twitter and other social accounts.

Sample Case

Through Social Media First Fruit Wellness Center Expands to Three Locations

One of the major challenges facing the most digital marketing campaigns is converting prospects into leads. However, First Fruit wellness had a distinctive and personal touch on social media marketing. By engaging with every follower, this Wellness center created close relationships with their prospects online.

The Challenge

The Wellness center needed to show their clients that they needed them. It needed to reach those prospects interested in improving their health and show the value of their service to the customers before they visited their center.

Many social media campaigns aim to achieve brand awareness. However, First Fruit Wellness center took things a notch higher by actively engaging its followers- finding out information about their health and goal, and encouraging them to visit the center and see how they can be helped.

For bigger companies, this interaction set up seems demanding, but for a brick-and-mortar organization like this wellness center, these kinds of personalized interactions eventually result to lead generation.

The Solution

Building Their Content Marketing

First Fruit Wellness center built an audience initially through content marketing. Engagement won't function without already existing followers. The first step the company took to creating social media campaigns was to curate sharable content, posting interesting content, and interacting with similar brands.

Connecting with followers Directly

When followers started connecting with the wellness center, the marketing team began interacting with them, immediately inquiring about their interests and goals.

This kind of personal interaction is quite rare in today's social media; therefore it not only served the purpose of creating strong relationships with customers but also showed them this brand was different.

Converting the Followers

The ultimate goal was lead generation–the marketing needed to get the followers to visit the center. When the relationship was strong enough, the First Fruit Wellness center convinced prospects to visit the center to learn more about the center and how it could help them out. By converting a lead in this way, about all the nurturing was done in online platforms.

Our Take

◆ In this era, most of your customers are on social media. They are not only searching for your brand and buying your products, but they also share opinions and experiences relating to your brand and business.

◆ So, you need to listen. Create an effective social media plan that will let you be part of the conversations taking place online, as well as interacting with your customers. If you want to increase your traffic, grow your leads, and increase your sales, it is high time to establish a social media presence—if you don't have one.

◆ However, a great social media plan is not a one-time thing; it's not set in stone. It is a constant and gradual process that requires you to make slight tweaks to your strategies every time. It's therefore important to learn how it works, so you can maximize it to grow your business and your audience.

Quiz 4

1. **A company wants to know if its influence growing. Which of the following is a significant influence growth?**

   a. Increase in the number of people leaving your website.

   b. Increases follower engagements.

   c. Employing a new customer support team

   d. Increase in the number of company influencers.

2. **Which once isn't an objective of Social Influencing?**

   a. Boost engagement with your content and products

   b. Increase web traffic

   c. Track your brand growth

   d. Grow your re-targeting list

3. **A new biscuit company is planning to adopt social listening. Which things should they watch out for?**

   a. Influencers

   b. Their Brand

   c. Topics relevant to their business

   d. Competitors

   e. All the above

4. _____ should handle content complaints.

    a. Product teams

    b. Content care teams

    c. Content teams

5. Which metric doesn't measure Social Listening efforts?

    a. Refund Rate

    b. Product Gaps

    c. Description of Earned Media Mentions

    d. Reputation

6. _____ is using social media to find, connect and convert leads.

    a. Social Listening

    b. Social Network

    c. Social Influence

    d. Social Selling

7. Why should an organization care for Social Selling?

    a. Their competitors are already using social selling

    b. To gain new customers and upsell existing customers

    c. None of the above

    d. All of the above

8. **Which Social Media metrics will help a company know where their traffic is coming from?**

    a. Direct Response Metrics

    b. Traffic by channel

    c. Offer Awareness

    d. Site engagement rates

9. **Companies and organization use _____ to boost brand visibility and encourage the use of devotion through authorities and marketers.**

    a. Search Engine Optimization

    b. Social Engine Marketing

    c. Social Networking

    d. Social Media

10. **Why is it so important for companies to establish a social media presence?**

    a. To foresee the future of the company

    b. To take advantage of their customer's online presence

    c. To create a goal and find a way to achieve them

    d. To increase their traffic, grow leads and increase sales

---

Solutions to the above questions can be downloaded from
the **Online Resources** *section of this book on*
www.vibrantpublishers.com

Chapter 5

Understanding E-mail Marketing

I n this era of social media, many can argue that the use of e-mail is irrelevant to marketing, but they are wrong. Why?

According to statistics.......

- At least 99% of people spend 5.4 hours per day going through their e-mails.

- For every dollar spent, e-mail marketing makes a $50 profit.

- About 60% of e-mail users say e-mails control their day-to-day purchasing decisions.

- While social media has a conversion rate of 1%, the e-mail marketing conversion rate is 2.3%.

When compared to social media, e-mails are superior, your targeted audience are most likely to check your e-mail message as opposed to social media.

You can post content on social media, but this doesn't mean that your targeted audience will want to see what you've posted. However, with e-mail, it's different because an e-mail stays in your inbox till it's read or deleted.

Yet, this doesn't mean you should abandon social media. It means you should use both marketing strategies simultaneously, by adding "Share" and "Like" buttons to your e-mail marketing messages. This gives your customers a way to interact and link with your brand, products, or services.

If done correctly, e-mail marketing will increase your sales substantially and boost your overall income. It's the best method to make your customers visit and return to your business website or blogs and increase traffic, which can result in increased conversion rates.

In this chapter, we will learn:

- What e-mail marketing is

- The role e-mail plays in digital marketing

- Ways of executing an e-mail marketing strategy effectively

- The different forms of e-mail marketing

- The metrics

5.1 Roles of E-mail Marketing

We already know what e-mail marketing is, but we don't know why it's very important for your business. And no, it's not for profit or growth, even though the outcome of a digital marketing strategy is increased sales and overall growth of the business.

The true purpose of e-mail marketing is to accelerate a customer's movement through the customer value journey. When the customer is traveling through this path, their lifetime value increases too, resulting in increased profit and stability of the business.

I don't think it will do us any harm to look at some other important aspects of e-mail marketing.

Communication Channel: Yes! It is true, about 99% of consumers look at their e-mails at least once a day. This is far much better than what other channels get.

Sole Owner of Your List: There are cases of businesses having their social media channels suspended or deleted for no reason; as a result, they lose all their contacts, fans, followers and posts. This is catastrophic, but with an e-mail list, your leads are yours.

E-mail Converts Better: E-mail marketing has an ROI of 4,400%. Wow! No social media converts better than that. The average purchases on e-mails are about three times higher than that of social media.

Measurable: You can always use e-mail marketing software to track your e-mails, you can know who opened it, the exact links clicked, and the number of unsubscribed people. This gives you a picture of how your digital marketing campaigns are performing; as a result, you can make the adjustments to improve its productivity.

Personal: What you're doing in e-mail marketing is segmenting your leads list and sending them e-mails tailored to resonate with their interests and preferences.

5.2 Methods of Well-Executed E-mail Marketing

Executing an e-mail marketing strategy can be very challenging for every type of business, regardless of its size. E-mail marketing is not just about sending announcements and promos to potential clients and customers.

You have to keep your audience engaged so they can look forward to your e-mails. This way, they can always keep your business in mind, even if they are not yet ready to purchase your product or services.

In simple terms....

You shouldn't be sending your customers the same e-mails all the time.

To be a pro at e-mail marketing, you need to understand the different e-mail types you can use to keep your subscriber entertained, and even boost your sales.

5.2.1 Types of Effective Marketing E-mails

1. Transactional E-mails

2. Relational E-mails

3. Promotional E-mails

Transactional E-mails

Transactional e-mails apply to transactions your business has with your customers. Also, they are used in requesting or sending updates on customer orders. Once a customer triggers specific actions, they receive an e-mail automatically in their inbox.

Here's is a list of transactional e-mails you can use in your e-mail marketing.

1. Order Confirmations

An order confirmation e-mail is a transaction e-mail notifying customer that you received or processed their orders. These e-mails contain crucial transaction data such as items purchased, the amount paid, and the delivery address.

It involves converting one-time customers into frequent buyers and frequent buyers into brand ambassadors. Your order confirmation e-mail should capture your customer's attention, eliminate confusion, and build the foundations of a long-lasting relationship with your clients.

2. Receipt E-mails

It's normal for an online store to send and receive receipts e-mails once a customer completes a transaction. Although it has a high open-rate, it cannot maximize business growth. They cannot create a great impression on their customers, smooth customer experience, or drive more revenue.

3. Account Creation

Customers receive this kind of e-mail when they create an account with your online business. It provides them with their login details.

Giving customers access to a small group is like presenting them with a gift. To leverage on it, you can ask your customers to share their happiness with their social media followers, hence boosting your brand awareness.

4. Sale Follow-ups

Let's say you're selling a physical product that can take time to reach your customers; it requires shipping. You can send your clients a bunch of post-transaction e-mails updating them on the status of their delivery from shipping, to delivery, and finally, arrival.

It's best to maximize these e-mails to boost your brand opportunities. Don't just send plain text order updates; include other necessary order information such as what the customer should do to receive their orders, or check their status, or contact information for customer support in case they have any queries.

5. Review Requests

Once you have sent a customer his/her purchase, and he/she's satisfied, you can send them an e-mail requesting them to send you a testimonial or review.

Amazon uses a simple visual presentation to solicit reviews from their customers. This kind of simplicity ensures that customers understand what is being asked of them. If the customer wants to write a review, he/she can click a link to the review image and he/she'll be directed to a page that allows him/her to leave his/her written review and star rating.

When you post the reviews or testimonials on your online store, third-party review websites, or social media platforms, it will serve as proof that can help you build trust and confidence among potential customers.

Relational E-mails

Relational e-mails deliver value to customers by offering free information such as newsletters, social updates, subscriber welcomes, and more.

Even though they may make an offer or sell a product or service directly, they build relationships with clients by adding value to your product or services (i.e., if you send your customer a high-quality e-newsletter, the customer is interacting more with your brand in a more meaningful way.

1. Newsletter

Newsletters are the most popular type of e-mails, with at least 83% of companies sending them to their e-mail list. Companies usually send based on a consistent schedule and often comprise content from the business websites, blogs, and links created from other sites.

A newsletter comprises updates on your products, upcoming webinars and events, and other new things about your products or services. Make sure every newsletter content you create is relevant and important to your prospects.

If you want to engage with the people in your e-mail list, a newsletter is the best campaign to send. It will keep your brand and products on it in the mind of your customers, driving them back to your site.

2. Survey E-mails

"A good e-mail marketing campaign isn't a monologue, rather a dialogue."

You don't want to be sending a bunch of e-mails to your subscribers without asking them what they think about your product or service. That's where surveying e-mails come into the picture.

They are very simple e-mails sent within a couple of weeks to ask customers to respond to certain questions related to topics relevant to your product or service.

3. Company E-mail Updates

Company e-mail updates create your brand awareness and presence in the market. Important updates such as new employees, new branding, press releases, new partnerships, and more are usually communicated to customers via e-mail marketing.

Perfect company e-mail updates present companies as dynamic, forever evolving, innovative, and constantly improving the products or services they provide.

4. New Content Announcement E-mail

These e-mails are marketing messages sent to people to inform them of new, changed, or updated content. They publicize new videos, e-books, podcasts, or blogs that have been recently published.

These are not the old boring type of sales e-mails; instead, they are interesting e-mails that ensure your audience stays informed on product updates, entertained, and educated.

5. Social Update

Social update e-mails update your business followers and customers on your product or service. This not only raises their excitement levels but keeps them in the loop on what to expect.

Promotional E-mails

These are the most used type of marketing e-mails, and they aim to make offers to your e-mail list leads. The offers can include a white paper, webinar, a brand announcement, a new product release, or promotional content. They boost your overall sales.

These marketing e-mails accomplish higher CTRs to the company's website, especially if the promotion exists only for a limited period.

1. Event Invitation E-mails

E-mails can be great avenues for promoting upcoming events, your business is hosting.

However, if you are inviting your e-mail list of contacts to register for an event, it's paramount to explain why it's attending the event is worth their time. The best way to do this is by using visuals that show your potential audience of why the event will be remarkable.

2. Co-marketing E-mails

These are e-mails designed as a partnership between two brands, allowing the business to market their offer to a shared audience. If done right, co-marketing e-mails increase audiences, boost conversions, and drive sales.

Sharing the same traits with e-mail marketing, co-marketing is the best place to create marketing campaigns.

3. Sale Announcement E-mails

These e-mails get more engagement than any other category of e-mails. If you want to increase your sales, use a subject line that will guarantee you're noticed by your subscribers.

4. Product Launch

Product launch e-mails are e-mails sent to a customer with the sole purpose of informing on new products, new releases, new features, and upcoming events. However, many clients rarely like receiving these e-mails, because they are not engaging or interesting like an offer. As a result, these e-mails should be simple and straightforward.

5. Special Offer E-mails

Special offer e-mails comprise discounts, coupons, and other interesting deals offered to customers on the VIP list. These e-mails have a very high opening rate, and most of the time, they improve your marketing ROI.

It's important to offer your subscriber special offers, as it's the best way to keep them engaged and, hopefully, it can result in a sale. Try to impact a sense of exclusivity and appreciation when sending these types of e-mails. This way, they can know they are part of your exclusive group.

5.2.2 The Phases of E-mail Marketing

Figure 5.1

By understanding the phases of e-mail marketing, you can curate and send the right message to your new subscribers at the right time.

The Indoctrination Campaign

This is a welcome campaign for your subscribers or prospects. It introduces your brand to them and clarifies who you are in their mind.

What it aims to achieve

- How your brand started
- What they can expect from you
- About your brand
- Where you're from
- What your position is

In this campaign, you must work as a marketing team to encourage the prospect to trust you and feel a connection with your brand.

The campaign will establish your authority and inform your prospects of what value you will provide them to make their lives better.

If you do a good job in this phase, they will most likely recognize your brand in their inbox and start engaging with you and the content you send them.

How to Go About It

- First, welcome the new subscriber and introduce them to your product or service.
- In bullet points, state the benefits they will receive as your subscribers.
- Explain to them what to expect from your brand.
- Encourage them to use your solutions.
- Send them the best of your work, stating that most of the subscribers have interacted with it and found it beneficial.

The Engagement Campaign

Think of this campaign more like a pursuit—even though your subscribers are still getting to know you.

This campaign acts as a follow-up to a lead-magnet subscription. Whether your lead magnet is a coupon of your product or a free e-Book download, send your e-mail message after the download to make your subscribers know that …

- They made an awesome decision by downloading your content.

- They can trust you.

- Why the lead magnet will benefit them.

What It Aims to Achieve

- Convert subscribers into buyers by recommending the next logical product they show interest in.

This campaign targets prospects who have already engaged with your brand. This way, you can engage with them, thank them for taking the action, and suggest the next product they are interested in and can end up with a sale.

How to Go About It

- Recognize their awesome decision.

- Attempt to address the thoughts and doubts they might experience that might prevent them from taking any action.

- Suggest the next appropriate step they should take.

- Ask them to purchase your product.

The Ascension Campaign

Once your e-mail subscriber buys your product, it triggers the ascension campaign. The campaign design allows you to start a customer value loop and turn a one-time buyer into a repeat buyer.

A customer "Value Loop Concept" increases buyers' frequency and lifetime value. For example, for every 100 buyers of your product, a percentage would buy your products again if you make them an additional offer.
The rate depends on:

- Your offer

- The way you describe it

- The temperature/state of traffic

If you clearly understand these, then you can always convert your one time consumer into a life-time consumer.

You already know what your customers love about your product, now it's time to make them crave for more and more of your products. Achieve this by reminding them of the benefits of your offer and increase their interests.

You can only achieve this by not taking your client for granted. Always offer them a product or service that will complement what they brought earlier. The fact is, this is the phase for making more money.

How to Go About It

- First, acknowledge the action they took by congratulating them.

- Address any doubts that might prevent them from taking the next step.

- State the next step they should take; hence, they can have a sense of direction.

No matter how impressive it is to increase your sales and make more profit, don't rush your clients. Don't push them too hard or they might feel uncomfortable and leave. That's a great loss for you.

If they aren't ready for the next step, don't push. Nurture them slowly until they are ready for your offer.

The Segmentation Campaign

This is the e-mail marketing campaign that you can send to your entire e-mail list.

Its created to….

- Help you segment your list further depending on the interests and preferences of your subscribers.

- Attract the interest of those subscribers stuck in their value journey.

You want your targeted audience to click or opt-in and be interested in the product and services you provide. Set up an engagement campaign to continue speaking to those subscribers who have opted in.

The campaign might be in the form of a promotion, so you need to study and figure out which subscribers has clicked, opened, and reacted to the message.

The promotional content might include:

- Lead magnets

- Blog posts

- Webinars

- Special offers

- Promos

Pick out those who click your e-mail messages and place them in a separate list (follow up on them later).

The Re-Engagement Campaign

If you're worried that your subscribers or customers aren't opening or reading your e-mails, then this campaign will suit you.

The re-engagement campaign can be used to:

- Call out inactive subscribers and get them reading your e-mails once again

- Get them interested in your brand

- Remind them of the benefits they are missing out

- Boost deliverability and decrease complaints

The fact is, some of your e-mails will not interest everyone on your list. And because of some circumstances or doubts, some of your active subscribers might become inactive.

By using this campaign, you can attract their interest in your product or service, and they will start engaging with your e-mails.

Use these strategies to speed up your customer's journey

Figure 5.2

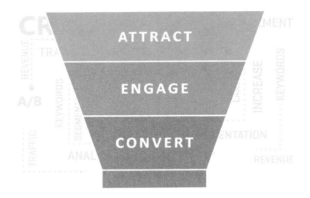

As we discussed earlier, e-mail marketing is all about expediting your customer journey. So, once a prospect shows interest in your brand and converts into a subscriber, you have to:

- Convert them into customers.

- Get them interested in your brand.

- Ascend them through the phases by making them purchase your high-quality products.

- Convert them into repeat-buyers.

- Convert them into brand ambassadors.

5.3 The Metrics to Measure E-mail Marketing

List Growth Rate

This metric track if your list is growing. Calculate it by subtracting the number of unsubscribes from your subscribers, then divide it by the total number of e-mail addresses, and finally multiply by 100.

It's normal to experience some challenges, but focus on growing your list, engaging your subscribers, and finding loyal subscribers.

Compliant Rate

This marks the percentage of spam complaints compared to the e-mails sent to subscribers.

Overall ROI

This metric tells you the overall ROI for your e-mail marketing campaigns. The metric is calculated by taking your income from your sales and subtracting the money spent to fulfill the campaign, divided by the money invested in the campaign, multiplied by 100.

E-mail marketing has the highest ROI out of any form of digital marketing strategy.

Open Rate

Open rate is the percentage of messages opened by subscribes compared to the number of e-mails sent out.

Click-Through-Rate (CTR)

This metric is the percentage of e-mails clicked compared to the number of e-mails sent, or the number of e-mails opened.

Our Take

◆ If you haven't been paying too much attention to e-mail marketing, now might be time to include it in your overall digital marketing strategy.

◆ E-mail marketing delivers a huge ROI for businesses and marketers that are willing to start. It's not that complicated.

◆ Because you're just a guest in a subscriber's inbox, it's good to remember that your e-mails are just one step away from losing their interest. You should, therefore, be respectful, polite, and your messages should deliver some value.

◆ Deliver on the promises you make. Provide your subscriber with what they have asked for, and not what you think is best for them. E-mail them regular messages that are in-line with their expectations.

◆ It might take some time to master some of the tactics we have mentioned in this chapter but putting all your time and effort into e-mail marketing is worth it. It will drive more leads and sales than any other strategy.

Quiz 5

1. **When creating subject lines for email campaigns, what should be considered?**

   a. Clear and Concise

   b. Brand name and inclusion

   c. Customer personalization

   d. All the above

2. **Why is it important to have a clear Call to Actions within your email message?**

   a. It provides clients direction on what to do as a result of receiving the email message.

   b. A CTA is not an important component of an email message.

   c. It provides clients with an overall view of your brand.

3. **What should your email message consist of?**

   a. Text only

   b. Image only

   c. A combination of images, text, and other tags.

4. **When writing messages for your email campaigns you need to ensure that?**

    a. That the email message addresses the needs of the recipient.

    b. That it has a reference to your brand.

    c. It doesn't meet the interest of the recipient.

5. **Every email message you send to your recipients should....**

    a. Should not contain a reference to your brand

    b. Should contain a physical Address and an Unsubscribe link.

    c. It should make it impossible for someone to unsubscribe for future messages.

6. **Which marketing emails types can help you build relationships with clients by adding value to your products?**

    a. Promotional Emails

    b. Relation Emails

    c. Transaction Emails

7. **What is the true purpose of Email Marketing?**

    a. To increase sales and overall growth of the business.

    b. To accelerate customer movement through the customer value journey.

    c. All the above

8. **The goal of an email message subject should….**

    a. Encourage prospects to open your email messages

    b. Tempt prospect to go through your email messages

    c. Tempt high-value targeted-customer to open, read, and act on your email message

9. **Which statement is wrong?**

    a. Re-Engagement campaigns call out subscribers and get them to read emails

    b. Re-Engagement campaigns get prospects interested in your brand

    c. Re-Engagement boost deliverability and decrease complaints.

    d. Re-Engagement increases your Return to Investment

10. **Which one of the following is not a metric to measure Email Marketing?**

    a. List Growth Rate

    b. Conversion from search

    c. Open Rate

    d. Click-through rate

Solutions to the above questions can be downloaded from
the **Online Resources** *section of this book on*
www.vibrantpublishers.com

This page is intentionally left blank

Chapter 6

Mastering Search Engine Marketing

Over the last few years, search marketing has radically changed for the better. Today, search marketing helps marketers increase their website traffic and leads, while still sustaining other digital marketing fields too.

Whether or not you are spending money on search marketing, you still want to make sure you reap the maximum benefits for your dime. That means you need an effective search marketing strategy.

There is so much traffic passing through Google and if you don't have the right marketing strategy, you lose a lot. Search engine marketing is a competitive business, and if you are depending on it to work without a strategy then be rest assured your competitors are not.

It's therefore critical to have a strategy, so you can take advantage of search as an acquisition channel and link it to other marketing efforts you might be undertaking.

In this chapter, you will learn:

- What search marketing is
- Characteristics of SEO
- The stages of a winning SEO
- The metrics

What is Search Marketing?

Search marketing is a digital marketing strategy that elevates websites by boosting their rankings and visibility on search engines (Bing, Yahoo, Google). It uses both organic (unpaid) and inorganic(paid) tactics to direct internet users to websites that will meet their needs.

6.1 Our Take On SEO

Figure 6.1

SEO can have ......

- **A Technical Side:** The focus here is on the technical details of a website, instead of the content.

- **A Content Side:** The focus here is on how to curate high-quality, optimized content, build links, and increase social shares.

Both categories must be used simultaneously for the success of the search marketing strategy. SEO content specialists will create content, build links, and get backlinks for your websites, but if Google cannot acknowledge these and you're not ranking, then you are most likely experiencing technical issues. As a result, you need an SEO technician.

SEO is a constant process.

You can't work on your SEO strategy just once and expect to rank higher in search engines. It's a continuous process of creating and updating your content and working on the technical aspects of your SEO.

It's important because your competitors are always working on their keywords to outdo you. If you don't work on your SEO continuously, you won't stay at the top for long.

Every time you overtake someone, there is always some else behind you working to over-rank you. This means your content needs to be updated and promoted every time to rank higher in Search Engine Result Pages (SERPS) and retain a top position.

Google's algorithm is rapidly changing.

Every month or year, Google changes its algorithm. With these changes comes new rules, which sometimes affect top ranking websites, especially if they used **black hat tactics** (*practices against search engine guidelines like cloaking, keyword stuffing and using private link networks*) to rank higher. Be ready to learn new strategies, always use **white hat tactics** (*practices that are in-line with the guidelines of major search engines*) on your SEO and follow the rules.

6.2 Methods of Well-Executed Search

Your search is mobile.

Mobile search is the new frontier in search marketing. Today, everyone is conducting their searches on their mobile devices. It's therefore important to make your website mobile-friendly to best capitalize on your search marketing strategy.

Your search is structural and technical.

You need Google to see you first before you can even start focusing on your SEO content and building links. The best way to achieve this is by creating better web pages than your competitors. Make sure your website appeals to your targeted audience's intent.

To make your page rank higher, find out what's already ranking for your target keywords, and create super-strong content that out-competes the existing one.

Your search uses "White Hat" tactics.

There are no easy buttons or hacks in SEO; you need to work hard. You need to follow all the rules provided by Google. They only want to provide the best search experience for their users.

Using **black hat or grey hat tactics** (*practices against search engine guidelines like cloaking, keyword stuffing and using private link network)* won't work, and if they work, they won't last for long. These tactics are unethical and most definitely illegal. Using the right tactics not only makes your business rank higher but also makes it look trustworthy and legit.

Your search is everywhere.

Google is probably one of the most famous search engines in the world, but it's not the only search engine. We have:

- Yahoo

- Bing

- Ask.com

- AOL search

- Belkko

- Web crawler

- Lycos

- Dogpile

All these channels have a search engine algorithm that you can take advantage of and maximize your success. So, you don't have to use Google only.

Furthermore, Google bots are complicated and smart; that's why companies have a hard time topping in their SERPS. However, Yelp and Pinterest search bots are less complicated and easier to use. The best part is, only a few people are competing on these channels, so you can easily reach the top.

Search engine marketing isn't just about Google, but about creating and publishing the right content to the right channels and doing what it takes to make your content rank higher, regardless of the channel.

Your search is more than traffic.

Yes, you have followed all the rules, you have ranked higher, and your traffic has exploded. But are you converting these visitors into leads? Are you making an income?

The whole purpose of marketing is to increase your income and achieve your business' financial and strategic aims by generating more leads and sales.

So, if you are ranking higher on Google searches and not converting, then all your efforts are being put to waste. Rethink your whole digital marketing strategy.

6.3 The Stages for a Winning SEO

Search marketing has three stages, and each stage has two priorities. Let's look at these stages and gain a deeper understanding of search engine marketing aspects.

Intent and Context

Behind every search, there is always an *intent*—the want or need—whether it's for a solution, more information, a product, or a service. Intent and context are both critical variables in search marketing. All brand engagement and sales funnel start with intent.

So, how do intent and context relate?

Usually, intent occurs inside the context of what Internet users are doing and what they're looking for or need. Understand the intent or context of the users before targeting a specific keyword.

Knowing the user context is vital in helping you craft content that provides solutions to the user's problem. Try to figure out what the user is looking for from your brand, product, or service. And why is it so important for the user to find that information?

You need to know how to anticipate the needs of the users. Find out the keywords they will most likely use to try to figure out the intent and context behind the searches.

Type your keyword into the Google search engine and look at the auto-suggestions; these suggestions are the most commonly searched keywords by people. From there, you can predict what they are looking for.

Intent and context research is something you need to understand so you can create long-term success with your SEO, keyword research, or search marketing strategy.

Asset and Channel

Now that you know what people are searching for and the reasons behind it, the next step is curate assets that will address those interests.

Create content that will address these questions:

- What intent are you targeting?

- What asset will address the search?

- Where will the asset live?

Your aim here is to select an asset that will address the intent or context of the people, then find a suitable channel for it to live on (YouTube, blog post, Pinterest).

Optimization and Ascension

The last stage is the optimization of your asset.

Once you have created your asset based on the intent or context of your prospect and you are ready to upload it, optimize it for the search algorithm, then build your lead ascension plan.

After you have attracted traffic to your site, you need to convert them to leads and sales. This will only happen if you provide your visitors with the steps they should take once they have seen your solution. Incorporate the steps in your asset.

Don't just optimize your content for search traffic—optimize for sales too. Pull traffic and convert it to leads and sales.

Here's how to optimize your page:

- Head to Google Analytics and find the pages on your website that rank top or has the highest traffic.

- Figure out the next logical steps for the traffic on those pages.

- Insert a CTA in the pages to lead your visitors to the next steps.

Search marketing aims to increase the traffic to your website, but that's not its main goal. Think of converting visitors into leads and guide them through the accession path to make them buy your product or services.

6.4 Metrics to Measure Search Marketing Strategies

Conversion from Search

If your site is an e-Commerce site, you can head to Google Analytics > Channel report and check out the top line income and the transaction number over time.

For example, if your report has over $67,000 from about 2100 transactions, you can calculate the conversion rate as $67,285.55/2130 which gives you $31.59/transaction.

Keyword Rankings

Use the SERPs Keyword rank-checker to track the positions of the keywords you want to use. Also, you can check out which of your competitors is outranking you. Check out their content and see what they are using that you are not, then update your content.

Traffic by Channel Report

Google Analytics allows marketers and business owners to understand where their traffic is coming from in detail. It also provides answers to a multitude of questions about traffic, although sometimes it might be too detailed to understand.

Google Analytics will tell if your traffic sources are balanced or not, whether it's coming from just one channel or multiple. Most websites that don't do search marketing receive their traffic from direct visits or e-mails. But once they implement social marketing, the distribution of their traffic becomes uniform.

Quality Backlinks

You can use tools like **Ahrefs, Moz Open Site Explorer,** and **MinitorBacklinks** for this metric. These metrics track the number of sites that are linking to your site.

Always run your reports monthly or quarterly to monitor how many sites are linked to your website. If your website is optimized, more and more quality sites will link to you.

Our Take

◆ Search marketing strategy is all about getting your products in front of your prospects or customers at that moment that they are searching for your products or services on Google or other search engines.

◆ However, search marketing isn't a one-time process. You will have to incorporate it with every element if your marketing, be it content creation, customer value optimization, or customer research.

◆ By using the methods discussed in this chapter, you fully leverage search marketing and outrank your competitors. Though it takes time and patience, you need to start. Over time, you will see an improvement in your page rankings and traffic.

Quiz 6

1. _____ is a digital marketing strategy that elevate websites by boosting ranking and visibility on search engines.

    a. Search Engine Optimization

    b. Search Marketing

    c. Search Engine Marketing

2. Which one is not a search engine?

    a. Bing

    b. Facebook

    c. Google

    d. Dogpile

3. Which one is not a search marketing stage?

    a. Optimizations and Ascension

    b. Intent and Context

    c. Awareness and Conversion

    d. Asset and Channel

4. **The following are ways to optimize your page which one is not?**

   a. Inserting a CTA in the pages to lead your visitors to the next steps

   b. Finding out the next logical steps for the traffic on your website pages

   c. Adding coupons to your websites to entice customers.

   d. Heading to Google analytics to find pages on your website that highest traffic

5. **Which tool cannot be used by a company to check their backlinks?**

   a. Ahrefs

   b. Google Analytics

   c. Monitor Backlinks

   d. Moz Open Site Explorer

6. **_____ practices against search engine guidelines like cloaking, keyword stuffing, and using a private link network.**

   a. Black Hat SEO tactics

   b. White Hat SEO tactics

   c. Grey Hat SEO tactics

7. **Which statement is correct?**

   a. SEO can have both a Technical and Content side

   b. SEO is a constant process

   c. SEO utilizes white hat tactics

   d. All the above

8. **Why are companies having a hard time rank higher in their SERPs?**

   a. They lack the right marketing team.

   b. Google Algorithms are constantly changing, and Google bots are complicated and smart

   c. Their content isn't interesting enough to the targeted prospects

9. **When should you run your reports to monitor how many sites are linked to your website?**

   a. Everyday

   b. Monthly or Quarterly

   c. At the end of the year

10. Which one is not a metric to measure search marketing strategies?

a. Conversion from search

b. Keyword Ranking

c. Click-through-rates

d. Quality Backlinks

Solutions to the above questions can be downloaded from the **Online Resources** *section of this book on*
www.vibrantpublishers.com

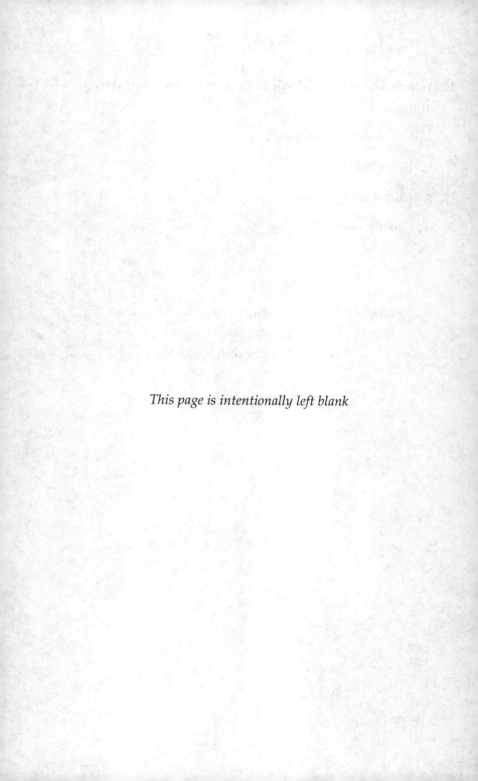
This page is intentionally left blank

Chapter 7

Key Metrics in Digital Marketing for Tracking and Measuring Success

In digital marketing, data and analytics help you track and measure the performance of different strategies. If you know how to interpret the numbers and convert them into actionable information, you can grow your business exponentially.

Yes, we have mentioned various metrics relating to various digital marketing strategies in the previous chapters, but they mostly focused on leads and conversion.

However, a successful marketing campaign is determined by much more, not conversions alone! There is traffic, sales-conversion, brand awareness, and much more.

In this chapter, we will learn:

- How to measure digital metrics successfully

- The key metrics for the success of your business

- How metrics works

But first, let's talk a little about data.

7.1 Why Data Is Important

Data can be enough, not enough, or too much.

But that's not the problem; the problem is understanding the data, converting the data into meaningful information, and making informed decisions based on them.

To understand what we are talking about, let's look at **Netflix** as an example.

Netflix

Netflix is the number-one video streaming company in the world. They believe that customization wins customers' loyalty; therefore, they have placed data at the center of all their strategies.

Back when they were still a DVD-renting company, they made huge investments in data mining technologies to create a movie recommendation algorithm, paving way for the use of data to create a better customer experience. Nearly 50 percent of their traffic resulted from recommendations.

This data approach didn't stop there. Today, **Netflix** uses customer's insights to create original content that appeals to their data-mined results, producing shows such as Stranger Things, The Punisher, and many more.

7.2 Categories of Metrics in Digital Marketing

Key Metrics: These are the metrics that evaluate the overall health of your business. You will know if a specific metric is a key metric when you look at it and immediately recognize if your business is doing well or not.

Drill-Down Metrics: They are more segmented; they help you to understand what's happening in specific areas of your organization.

Both categories of metrics work simultaneously. If a key metric tells you there is something wrong with your business, the drill-down metric will help you find the specific problem and you can fix it.

7.3 Measuring Your Digital Marketing Metrics Successfully - Make It

Even though data collected from marketing metrics can provide you with graphics, it may leave you without a clue on how to analyze your campaign and optimize it. Because of this, you need direction on how to choose and measure your digital marketing metric.

Here's How to Go About It:

Create Your Goals

Coming up with S.M.A.R.T. goals will spare you long hours of thinking.

- Specific: Are your goals detailed?

- Measurable: Can the goal be measured?

- Achievable: Can they be attained?

- Relevant: Are your goals in line with your short-term and long-term objectives?

- Timely: When are you supposed to achieve these goals?

You need to understand what you aim to accomplish, and with the help of SMART goals, measuring your digital marketing effort will become easy.

When you understand which metrics matter, you can give it your utmost attention. If you are after conversions, your attention will be on CPA and CPC because you will want to see the financial effectiveness of your marketing campaign.

Select Your Tools

There are a lot of paid and free web analytics tools you can use to measure your digital marketing metrics. Even though Google Analytics is the most popular tool, many businesses also use strategy-specific analytics tools, such as Ahrefs and MinitorBacklinks for SEO.

Choose Your Reporting Method

Creating a report even before you launch your digital marketing strategy can save you lots of time. Also, you can focus on the specific aspects you're measuring throughout the campaign period.

To build your report, you will need a program or channel. Google Data Studio is one of the famous free programs you can use. This program will help you and your marketing team to bring in data from Google Analytics and present it in an easy and informative way.

7.4 Digital Marketing Metrics You Need to Track and Measure

Many digital marketing metrics can track and measure the success of digital marketing campaigns. Below is a list of the most important metrics you need.

7.4.1 Traffic Metrics

Total Site Visits

The total site visit is the overall traffic metric used to track and monitor how many people have visited your site over time and how effective is your marketing campaign at driving traffic to your site. You can break it up into a medium, which describes where the traffic is coming from.

How to measure:

- Go to Google Analytics Dashboard
- Find the Acquisition Report
- Head to overview
- Go through the session column on the table

Tracing your overall traffic might aid you in figuring out a pattern that may put you in front of your competitors. If your digital marketing campaign is successful, your total traffic from all the sources should grow over time; if it falls month to month, it's time to rethink your marketing strategy.

1. Channel-Specific Traffic

These metrics determine which channels your traffic originates from. It segments your channels to pinpoint in which ones your full- scale digital marketing campaigns excels and in which one it does not.

Channels to Watch

Direct Visitors: These are the people who visit your site by inputting your URL in their browsers.

Organic Search: These visitors arrive at your website by performing a search on a search engine and clicking your website link in the organic search result.

Referrals: These people visit your website by clicking a link on another website. They are external traffic.

Social: Visitors arrived at your site through social media sites. This is the best indicator to measure the overall effectiveness of your social engagements, integrated campaigns, content, and SEO.

2. Mobile Traffic

With the widespread use of mobile devices for content consumption, it would be wise to track and monitor your mobile visitor's metrics, so you can understand your mobile customers and increase your conversion rate.

What you need to know:

- What's your mobile traffic rate?

- Which type of mobile devices and browsers do your visitors use?

- Where is your traffic coming from?

- What types of content are they consuming?

Websites with slow load times affect mobile metrics. If your site has the same problem, work on improving it so you can enjoy better conversion rates.

3. New Visitors vs. Number of Return Visitors

If the number of visitors returning to your site is higher, it shows that your website contains quality content that makes your visitors crave for more. Monitoring the ration of new visitors' vs returning visitors for weeks or months will help you track the performance of your new content.

For example, if the ratio of new visitors to returning visitors is higher compared to the previous week or month, it might indicate that your new content is relevant enough to drive new traffic to your site. However, if the ratio of returning visitors is low, then your site doesn't meet their needs.

4. Interactions Per visit

This metric provides a detailed report of your website, but if you know how to interpret it, you will gather valuable insight about your site. Some variables that you might want to look into including the number of pages visited by a user, the time they spend on a page, and the activity they do on the specific pages.

The analysis of your visitors' interactions with your website per visit gives you the chance to discover their interests and preferences, so you can deliver more content that can appeal more to them.

5. Time on Site

Time on site describes the average time a user spends on your website. It gives you insights on how a user interacts with your website. From the information gathered, you can measure the performance of your site.

If your visitors spend more time on your websites, it indicates that your content is interesting and valuable to the visitors. These visitors are most likely to convert into loyal customers.

By knowing the time spent by visitors on your site, you can optimize your content for the customers to convert them into devoted customers.

6. Bounce Rate

This metric measures the number of people who visit your site, but leave instantly, performing no meaningful task. A higher bounce rate sometimes means there are some critical issues in your digital marketing campaigns or website that need to be addressed.

Some issues include:

• Irrelevant traffic sources

• Poor digital marketing campaigns

• Weak landing pages

The bounce rate of every single page in your site can be different.

Maybe the guest visited the site and found the information he/she needed on the page and saw no need to go any further. Or maybe he/she called in and purchased your product after bouncing off your contact page.

How to Track ...

Bounce rate on your website:

- Open Acquisition > All Traffic > Channels
- Select the specific channels with high performance
- Look at the bounce rate

On Individual Pages:

- Head to behavior
- Open site content
- Select either Landing Pages or All Pages
- Look at the bounce rate column

7. Exit Rate

This is a very crucial metric for websites with multi-page conversion. Don't confuse exit rate and bounce rate. Exit rate tracks and measures the percentage of visitors who have left your website after exploring multiple times. This metric enables you to gain some insights into the buyer's journey and how to optimize your website accordingly to increase your conversion rates.

8. Cost Per Visitor (CPV) and Revenue Per Visitor (RPV)

CPV and RPV provide you with the formula for measuring the profitability of each marketing channel. If your RPV is higher than CPV, your marketing channels are profitable. They also help in the budgeting of certain types of paid marketing campaigns.

CPV estimates how much each ad costs a marketer. It's calculated as a total investment per channel divided by the number of visitors generated.

RPV is the measurement of the income generated each time a customer visits your site. It's calculated as total revenue divided by the total number of visitors on your site. It's a method of estimating the value of each additional visitor.

So, if your revenue per month is $10,000, and your site receives 1,000 visitors, then your RPV will be $10,000/1,000 or $10 per visitor.

7.4.2 Conversion Metrics

Not so long ago, the conversion was the process by which a person evolved from visiting your site into a customer. But today, marketing is all about tracking the interests and engagement of your customers on your site to get them deeper into the marketing funnel.

A visitor is converted when he/she triggers certain desired actions like clicking the download button, signing up for a trial, filling out a form, or creating an account.

In simple terms…

Conversions are the number of unknown visitors who become recognized and included in your marketing database.

1. Total Conversions

If your site receives lower conversions, it means there are several problems. Maybe your website design is poor, or your offers are unattractive, or your visitors are disinterested. Either way you need to address them.

Monitoring your conversions helps you pinpoint which variables your visitors are interacting with on your site and which ones are useless. If you are experiencing low conversion rates, it's time to update or upgrade your **UX** (*user experience)* and other important components of your website.

How to view:

- Head to conversions

- Go to Goal > Overview

- Hit "View full report"

2. Micro Conversion Rates

This metric involves tracking the "micro" conversions or conversions at the campaign level, to ensure that the smaller Key Performance Indicators (KPIs) are accounting for your overall digital marketing strategy.

For example, if you have higher conversion rates supporting a lead magnet, but you have only a few leads moving to the next step of the marketing funnel, then there is a problem. You may receive higher conversion rates, but your leads are not advancing. As a result, you're not achieving your overall marketing goals.

3. Conversion Funnel Rates

The Conversion Funnel Rate is the percentage of potential customers moving through each stage of the funnel successfully, and their behaviors or interests show they're still willing to move even further. This metric gives you a deeper understanding of how each step of the marketing funnel affects your ROI and where to concentrate your resources.

4. Click-Through-Rates (CTR)

This is one of the most important metrics in e-mail marketing, paid ads, and SEO campaigns.

Paid media CTR determines the quality score, which affects the cost-per-click and ads position.

Also, it's one of the best ways to determine which ads and keywords are appealing to customers. High CTR can lower the cost per click, while lower CTR can dramatically increase the cost per click.

E-mail *marketing CTR* enables e-mail marketers to monitor and evaluate the effectiveness of an e-mail message. A high CTR indicates impressed and interested e-mail readers who are clicking the link to your website.

SEO organic CTR influences how your website is ranked. Search marketers can influence organic CTR by using page titles, URLs, and descriptions with relevant keywords and interesting copies that can appeal to the users.

Ways to Increase your CTR:

- Trying different ad copies

- Curating attractive offers

- Optimizing landing pages

When changing your ad campaigns, observe any sudden increase or decrease in CTR. A significant increase could signal a perfect marketing campaign. A sudden decrease could show a problem in your campaign.

5. New vs. Returning Visitor Conversions

The engagement of a new visitor on your site differs greatly from the way regular visitors behave. By tracking these numbers, you can identify new useful insights for reducing bouncing rate, increasing return visitor numbers, boosting conversions, and maximizing customer lifetime value. Try to use marketing automation and upselling to achieve this.

7.4.3 Revenue Metrics

Cost Per Lead

This metric helps you in finding out the cost you're spending to convert a visitor to your site.

Developing a cost per lead analysis is searching for all factors involved in generating the lead. They comprise:

- The cost for a particular PPC campaign

- The number of visitors on your landing page giving you their contact information

A campaign is only successful when the cost per lead is lower than the average amount a customer spends. The lower your cost per lead, the higher your revenue. If you don't know how much it costs you to gain a lead, then you are at a loss.

Once you know the cost of an average lead, you can use different new methods to find cost-effective methods, gain more leads, and maintain your current source of leads.

ROI

Return on investment determines your total revenue from your digital marketing strategies. It compares the amount of money you invested in your strategies to the amount of money you have earned from them.

A negative ROI results from a high bounce rate and low conversion rates. Your digital marketing will only succeed if your ROI is positive.

Our Take

◆ Data and analytics can be easily understood, especially if you know how to intercept them. You can use them to identify opportunities and red flags in your marketing.

◆ Understanding metrics gives you confidence in your marketing strategies.

◆ With the help of the above digital marketing metrics, you and your marketing team can measure the impact of your overall digital marketing strategy. You can also fix any issues affecting the performance of your strategy.

◆ The changes will influence your digital marketing metrics, as well as your revenue.

Quiz 7

1. **How can you best define the term Metrics?**

   a. A benchmark

   b. A standard of measurement

   c. Process of measuring

   d. All the above

2. **Channel Specific Traffic is a metric that determines on which channel traffic originates from.**

   a. True

   b. False

3. **Which of the following best describes Key Metrics?**

   a. Are metrics that help you understand what's happening in specific areas of your organization.

   b. Are the metric that evaluates the overall health of your business.

   c. Are metrics that track and monitor how many visitors have visited your site.

4. **In the list below, which one is not among the most common metrics used to measure traffic?**

   a. Mobile traffic

   b. Cost per lead

   c. Interaction per visit

   d. New Visitors Vs Number of Return Visitors

5. **Which of the following is the best way to measure conversion?**

   a. ROI

   b. Time on site

   c. Interaction per visit

   d. Total Conversion

6. **Companies with the best way to track and measure their data outperform their competitors in which of the following.**

   a. Lead generation and sales growth

   b. Profitability

   c. Increased conversion rates

   d. All the above

7. **Which of the following statements better reflect the importance of digital marketing metrics?**

   a. Gives marketers confidence in their marketing strategies and a way to measure the impact of digital marketing strategies.

   b. Allow marketers to effectively count the results of campaigns

   c. Allows marketers to better predict the outcome of their marketing strategies

8. **Which of the following best defines Conversion Funnel Rates?**

   a. It's the percentage of potential customers moving through each stage of the marketing funnel successfully.

   b. It's a metric that measures micro-conversion and conversions at the campaign level to ensure KPIs are accounting for the overall marketing strategy.

   c. It tracks and measures the percentage of visitors who have left your website after exploring it multiple times.

9. **Which one is not part of the SMART goal?**

   a. Specific

   b. Measurable

   c. Achievable

   d. Re-targeting

   e. Timely

10. _____ it provides you a detailed report about your website.

   a. Time on site metric

   b. Interaction Per Visit Metric

   c. Mobile traffic

   d. Bounce Rate

Solutions to the above questions can be downloaded from the **Online Resources** *section of this book on* **www.vibrantpublishers.com**

This page is intentionally left blank

Chapter 8

Taking Advantage of Conversion Rate Optimization (CRO)

About 75 percent of businesses are unhappy with their conversion rates. Although this might be a reassuring sign of awareness, it also means that converting guests into customers is a major difficulty facing most companies.

To avoid being part of the many unhappy businesses, make conversion rate optimization (CRO) a core part of your digital marketing strategies. By supporting your CRO strategy, you can drive more traffic to your site, grow your leads, and convert more visitors into committed customers.

Is CRO about converting visitors into customers?

Yes and no. You see, not all websites are created to attract new customers; some are built to be media-driven or informative. This means they can count "newsletter subscriptions" or "video views" as conversion.

Based on a website's primary objective, we can say CRO is about turning passive visitors into active visitors in a way that meets the marketing objectives of a business.

The only way to increase your conversion rates is by learning how to communicate effectively and developing positive experiences, so your site visitors can trigger actions that will convert them to leads.

In this chapter, we will learn:

- What CRO is

- The benefits of CRO

- How to use CRO effectively

- The metrics to measure CRO

8.1 What is Conversion Rate Optimization (CRO)?

CRO involves reviewing your website's marketing funnel to establish the best strategy you can use to increase your leads ratio.

This process involves using analytical techniques in your conversion strategies to help you boost your site conversion rates. But first, you need to determine your brand's target, and then make informed choices that will optimize your website objectives, resulting in increased conversions.

To better optimize your CRO, you need to have a deeper understanding of the behaviors of your website's users and visitors, and also figure out if there is any action or operation on your website that can cause them to leave without converting into leads.

The information you'll gather will give you insights on how to create an effective website optimization procedure that will eventually increase your conversion rates and boost your business growth.

8.2 Why Is CRO So Important?

CRO is important because it helps you to create more leads and boost your sales using existing traffic. You don't have to pay any additional money for advertising, because you will be using your existing traffic to create additional money.

Besides helping to convert existing traffic to customers and gain leads, CRO provides many additional benefits.

Here are a few benefits.

Helps You Create Additional Income with the Existing Traffic

If you're having high conversion rates from your existing sources of traffic sources, it means you're making an additional income. How?

Let's say you have experienced a 10-percent rise in your conversion rates, the increased ratio will equate to additional income. So, 10% of 10,000 leads equal to 1000. If you're selling your product at $50 per download, it means that you're getting an additional $50 * 1000 new leads, which equals 50,000 more incomes.

Note: The conversion rate is cost effective because you are

utilizing your current website traffic to generate more revenue. As a result, you're not paying extra cash to make more cash.

From this, you can see that the conversion rate is a vital element of digital marketing strategy.

Relegates Cost of Customer Acquisition

Because CRO is cost-effective, it lowers the cost of customer acquisition by mobilizing your existing traffic to create new leads.

So, if your landing pages convert visitors at the rate of 15% per 10,000 web traffic/month, that means you're gaining 1,500 new leads every month. However, if you optimize your landing page and produce 20 percent new leads, this will result in an additional five percent or 500 leads.

Now let's assume the additional 500 leads buy your product at $50 each, which will result in $50*500 leads, which gives 25,000 extra revenues from the same traffic. Hence, you can make more money from your current customers and boost your business faster by tweaking your CRO techniques.

Website CRO Lets You Focus on Vital Web Traffic

CRO must be part of your digital marketing strategy because it helps you direct your efforts to the part that matters a lot in your marketing campaigns. That's digital assets and they are responsible for your website traffic.

So, rather than focusing your effort on your entire website, you can focus them on those specific areas that transform your traffic to customers and leads. Consequently, you'll be able to optimize your web pages that are not converting traffic effectively.

8.3 How to Perfectly Execute CRO

Your website is already receiving tons of traffic, but very few are converting.

What is wrong?

There are so many issues that can cause a low conversion rate, and we covered most of them in the previous chapters. Nevertheless, there is one thing that stands out: "optimization." By optimizing your website, you can improve the conversion rate of the traffic you already have.

Optimization is a continuous, dynamic, iterative process, and not a one-time activity. As long as you're trying to improve your results, you will repeat the optimization process repeatedly. It's like a loop.

In this section, we describe how the CRO loop works in different stages.

1. Create Your Goals

The first stage is to create your own SMART and unique goals/ objectives. What is it you're trying to achieve? If you have an objective, you can easily optimize it.

Let's say you want to optimize your homepage.

A homepage is one of the most important pages on a website. It makes the first impression on your visitors; it guides them further into your website; it provides them with links to product information, and finally, it gives them a way of reaching you.

A homepage contains spaces for both your marketing team and the acquisition team.

In short, a homepage is a place where your visitors check out if your brand will meet their needs, and if so, where are they and what's the next step.

You can optimize your visitor's experience on your homepage using these three types of goals.

- An immediate goal: On-page form completion.

- A campaign goal: Links to purchase or lead magnets

- A long-term goalL Your lead quality, average order quality, or net value.

2. Collect Data

Once your goal is set, you need to find analytical tools to collect data. Data is important in digital marketing; you can't afford to make any business decisions based on assumptions.

You need to track and monitor metrics that align with your primary business goals so you can use them to make informed decisions later.

Wondering where to get your data?

- Google Analytics will contain metrics relating to your site.

- Analytic tools like TruConversion will track user behavior.

- Use payment processors like PayPal for payment data.

- Tools like Infusionsoft, Convertkit, will measure your customer and e-mail data.

If you find any issues, list them down and then find the most effective way to fix them so they don't occur again.

3. Examine Data

For a successful CRO, you must use the relevant data you've collected to build effective optimization strategies.

Examine your data and determine…

- Your conversion rate by using CRM or analytics data

- The cause of the low conversion rate by analyzing user behavior data

- Why and How the cause comes about by building a hypothesis (in the next stage)

Create a Hypothesis

This stage marks the start of the optimization process.

Without a hypothesis, you won't be able to optimize because you won't know what you are trying to solve or improve.

Once you have gathered the data analyzed and figured out what's affecting your conversion rates, you need to make some assumptions on how to solve the specific issues you have pinpointed.

All these might seem complicated, but it's simple. The hypothesis should contain these three components.

- The approach you plan to test.

- Who is being targeted by the approach?

- The expected outcome.

Your hypothesis represents your intent. Your outcome must be specific. Also, you need to be sure you can measure it and it's something you can use to solve your problem or better your results in a particular way.

Design Test

Armed with your hypothesis together with your data, you can create variables that you can test out. However, creating tests, setting them up, and running them can take time.

Additionally, you can only run a few tests in a site that receives low numbers of traffic, because the tests take too much time to run and you may never receive valid results on a small website.

So, if your website doesn't receive lots of traffic, don't run over 29 tests in a year. Just select the right test to run and try to perfect your skills in identifying and justifying the pages you want to optimize.

4. Implement Test Technology

Once you have all your variable set, implement all the technology necessary to make the changes you are testing. You need the right technology to complete this process. Some tools you can use include Google Analytics and Visual Website Optimizer.

5. Running the Tests

It's important to know when you should run your test and when you shouldn't. You first need to qualify your test to determine if you *can* run it.

A test should run until it achieves its "statistical significance." If it doesn't, then you will receive irrelevant or incomplete results. However, the statistical relevance of the test depends on the number of variables being tested and the number of conversions per day.

So, what's statistical significance?

We can define it as the mathematical way of proving if a test result is relevant. So, if you put a stop to your test early, you won't have enough data from the rest of the test to determine if your hypothesis was true. Maybe it was true or not, but you won't know if the test is not complete.

Besides, you can only get relevant results if you have enough required samples (traffic); lack of traffic means no data.

However, if your results show signs of being broken or failing, stop it and try to find out what is wrong.

It's your role as a conversion rate optimizer to lessen the risks while running tests on various ideas. There are some instances you can allow the test to run even if it's performing badly. This is when your traffic is from organic sources and you can afford to keep it running. But if your traffic it's from paid sources, you can't afford to keep the tests running, because you will be losing money.

To know if it's worth running a test or not, use this test:

- Is this an efficient issue with clarity in the result? If it's just an vague issue with no importance whatsoever, don't test.

- Does this page impact your long-term strategies directly? Yes! Run the test.

- Do you have something else that has a bigger effect on your business? Yes! Test it instead.

- Are these findings applicable to other areas of your site? No! Choose wisely. It's more helpful to run tests that impact two or more pages on your site.

- Do you have the resource to run the test? No! Don't waste your time then.

6. Analyze the Data

The last stage involves analyzing the results of your test. This way, you'll be able to answer the "Why" and "How" and get new insights for your next campaign.

In this stage, you'll perform five important tasks, namely:

- Share lifts or losses
- Find the "Why" or "How"
- Create a report
- Record your data
- Share the results with other investors

Your report should comprise:

- The test name

- The time it took

- Metrics

- The variants

- Broken down long-form numbers

During the evaluation process, try to answer the answers below:

- What did you see: a lift, loss, or null?

- Did the result go against the hypothesis? If so, why?

- Is there a reason for retesting? Maybe the results are questionable because of various reasons.

- Can the data be used for future experiments? If it's yes, how?

The answers to these questions will help you create new objectives and start the whole process again.

Testing and optimizations should be an integral part of your digital marketing strategies. Every test you run should give rise to another test, and so on. The results from the tests will help you understand how to increase your conversion rate and grow your business significantly.

8.4 The Metrics

Optimization is all about numbers. So, which metrics matter a lot in conversion rate optimization?

1. Conversion Rate

This is the ratio of users and visitors to your website who have to undertake certain desired actions and attain your primary aim of conversion. It's calculated as the number of conversions divided by the total number of visitors to the page you're testing.

Here is how you can calculate the ratio or percentage of conversion rates:

If you have 500 leads, divide it by 10,000 website visitors, then multiply by 100, which gives you five percent.
500/10,000 *100 = 5%.

2. Lift Percentage

This is the percentage change between multiple variables.

3. Conversion Range

Conversion rate is a misleading term; it implies that you only get one value called the "Conversion Rate," but in reality, it is more like conversion within a range.

Our Take

◆ A conversion optimization rate might sound like a mystery to new digital marketers—but it's a simple, effective way to optimize your site and find pages that require optimization.

◆ If you keep on testing your pages, you will find out what's working and what's not. Subsequently, you will make the necessary changes to perfect your marketing campaigns and grow your business.

◆ If you want to increase conversion rates, you need to begin with optimizing your pages. Smart businesses use CRO to empower their websites and stores to generate a massive increase in conversions and sales.

Quiz 8

1. **Which of the following can be optimized when operating CRO?**

    a. The Website

    b. Company Ads

    c. The Lading page

    d. All the answers are correct.

2. **What Describes a landing page better?**

    a. A landing page is an image

    b. A landing page is a page on social media

    c. A landing page is a web page that appears by clicking on an online ad or a search engine search.

    d. A landing page is a marketing brochure

3. **How does increasing conversion rate affects an organization?**

    a. It helps an organization gain more leads

    b. It helps the company's social media

    c. It reduces visitors

    d. It helps an organization employ more efficient managers

4. **Which of the following formulas is used to calculate conversion rates?**

   a. Revenue by number of visitors

   b. Number of visitors by revenue

   c. Number of conversion divide by the total number of visitors

   d. The number of visitors divided by the number of orders

5. **Which of the following activities will you not perform when analyzing data?**

   a. Share lift or loses

   b. Test name

   c. Record data

   d. Create a report

6. **_____ is a mathematical way of proving if a test is relevant.**

   a. Conversion optimization rate

   b. A/B testing

   c. Statistical significance

   d. Conversion Range

7. **Why is CRO important?**

   a. It lets you direct your effort to the parts that matter a lot in your CRO.

   b. Because your taking traffic that may or may not convert and turning them to actual revenue.

   c. Because it's cost-effective and lowers customer acquisition

   d. All the above

8. **Which step is not part of the CRO loop?**

   a. Building Goals

   b. Collection of Data

   c. Creating a hypothesis

   d. Scripting

9. **Which of the following defines the process of Conversion Optimization?**

   a. Making frequent changes to your website layout and see if sales improve.

   b. Making many small changes to your site and see the results

   c. Making small progressive variations in your website over time and seeing which variation has the highest performance.

   d. Making numerous big changes instantly to see which change has the fastest result.

10. **Which two are the central pillars of business success for Conversion Optimization success?**

   a. Marketing and customer focus

   b. User experience and sales

   c. Continuous improvement and marketing

   d. Customer focus and continuous improvement

Solutions to the above questions can be downloaded from the **Online Resources** *section of this book on*
www.vibrantpublishers.com

NOTES

CPSIA information can be obtained
at www.ICGtesting.com
Printed in the USA
LVHW060717170723
752609LV00001BA/6